Endorsements

"…a fresh and winning focus on the challenge of recovery — a struggle that impacts millions of lives. *Recovering Me, Discovering Joy* reveals the cockeyed maze we sometimes must walk to finally reach the deeply embedded roots of addiction. Using her own struggles with anxiety and depression as an example, Vivian reveals how to surrender by using a faith-based approach to healing the body and the soul."

Carol Sveilich, MA, Award-winning author of *JUST FINE: Unmasking Concealed Chronic Illness and Pain* and soon to be released: *JUST FINE: Unmasking Depression and Anxiety Disorders*

"Vivian has selflessly shared her multiple inner struggles in order to help others. She talks about very difficult subjects with heart-warming good humor and shares her faith as an integral part of recovery. Anyone in recovery, or close to someone who is, will benefit from this book."

Dave Carey, Motivational speaker and author of *The Ways We Choose: lessons for life from a POW's experience*

"Vivian's book is not just for those in 'recovery.' It is essential reading to assist anyone who is creating a quality life in these challenging, changing times."

Dorothy Mitchell, MSCCP, Professor Emeritus Long Beach City College; California State University Long Beach; University of Hawaii

---

"A treasure filled with guidance and encouragement."

Greg S Reid, The Millionaire Mentor and best selling author, www.AlwaysGood.com

---

"…heartfelt, honest, and inspirational this book is amusing, touching, sincere, infusing hope and encouragement for any reader. Vivian shares her spiritual beliefs without sounding preachy."

Karen Sommerfeld-Forge, Ph.D., Program Manager, Palomar Outpatient Behavioral Health

---

"*Recovering Me, Discovering Joy* is a well-written, fresh, and revealing personal story of a journey from depression, anxiety and alcoholism into joy, faith and recovery. It is a helpful guide to uplift and inspire readers going through any challenging time. Vivian gently reminds us that we are not alone in any struggle."

Judy Saalinger, Ph.D., MFT, CAS, Lasting Recovery Outpatient Alcohol and Drug Addiction Treatment Center, author of *FEARLESS CHANGE, Embrace the Choice to Reinvent Your Life*

Recovering Me, Discovering Joy is a brave and heartwarming book. Vivian writes honestly of her struggles and triumphs, empowering readers with wisdom, information, and motivation to let go of victimhood and embrace a joy-filled life. This book will inspire anyone who wants to improve their health and their quality of life.

Lynne Klippel, author of *Web Wonder Women*

Recovering Me Discovering Joy

Recovering Me
Discovering Joy

Uplifting Wisdom for Everyday Greatness

Vivian Eisenecher

KTW Publishing
San Diego, California

This book contains general information and is not intended to be, nor should be, used as a substitute for specific medical advice. It is recommended that you consult a healthcare professional before undertaking any medical protocol or exercise program.

Names and identifying characteristics of certain individuals included in this book have been changed to protect their identities.

Eisenecher, Vivian.
    Recovering me, discovering joy : uplifting wisdom for everyday greatness / Vivian Eisenecher.
    p. cm.
    Includes bibliographical references and index.
    LCCN 2008901254
    ISBN-13: 978-0-9814871-5-1
    ISBN-10: 0-9814871-5-7

1. Self-actualization (Psychology)
2. Self-actualization (Psychology) – Religious aspects.
3. Recovering addicts – Psychology.   I. Title.

BF637.S4E37 2008   158.1
                        QBI08-600111

Dedicated to my Mom
who lived before there were therapies to help her

To my wonderful children, Kim and Todd

To my husband, Bill, for his love and encouragement

To those who still suffer from depression, social anxiety
and/or alcoholism–may you find support and proper treatment

And finally to all who have spoken to my heart
and helped me find my way.

Table of Contents

PART TWO – DISCOVERING JOY

Acknowledgements

My sincere thanks to:

Geoff Whyte, my editor, for taking my thoughts and words and making them grammatically correct. www.whyteink.com.au

Ken Colby for his creative photography and his can do attitude. www.greenscreenwizard.com

Chris Chase and Orville Esoy of Chris Chase Design for putting together one fine book cover. www.ChrisChaseDesign.com

The Color House Graphics crew for typesetting, printing, fulfillment and for making my life infinitely less stressful. www.colorhousegraphics.com

All my readers, around the globe—past, present, and future. May you find joy wherever life leads you.

Introduction

Recovering Me, Discovering Joy is for anyone who has ever had to forge ahead after a negative life event. If you have ever had to bounce back from a failed relationship, convalesce from an illness, recoup any kind of loss, or just recover from a bad day, then this book will be beneficial. It will help you with your recoveries, and it will help you move on to live a richer, easier and happier life.

Recovering Me, Discovering Joy takes a good honest look at how I, my husband and countless others have used recovery not as a disadvantage, but as an opportunity and springboard to an improved life. We learned that it's not about recovering to normal – it's about recovering to a *better* normal...from anything.

This book is about my transformation from a depressed, anxiety-laden alcoholic to a successful, grateful and joyful woman. For me, it took my total collapse and complete failure to finally understand that I wasn't just battling alcoholism, I was fighting two other distinct disorders as well. Believe it or not, this realization paved the way for me to finally enjoy life. Until then, my life had been a struggle, an uphill climb within the grim-looking landscape of my mind. My newfound love for life was such a complete turnaround that, to benefit others, I wanted to commit to paper pivotal parts of my journey.

It took the diagnosis and *successful* treatment of not only alcoholism but also my chronic low-grade depression, called dysthymia, and my social phobia or S.A.D. (Social Anxiety Disorder) for me to recognize that these two lifelong disorders were 'triggers' for my alcoholism. They were the ugly underbelly of the beast. Substance abuse was a mere symptom of two underlying disorders that were not discernible to anyone, not even me.

All my life, I had wondered why everything seemed so hopeless, why my life seemed so meaningless, and why I was unable to experience any real joy. Along with that, I had a deep, lifelong fear of encountering people who I deemed 'better' than me (anyone with more money, better educated, etc.). Even though I had never known anything different, somehow I knew the way I felt wasn't right. I had no idea that I was depressed and anxiety-ridden until I was curiously (and serendipitously) treated for both conditions.

Because dysthymia and social phobia don't usually manifest in blatant negative symptoms or behavior, they are very good at evading the detection of medical professionals, forcing many sufferers to wallow in their misery, sometimes for their entire lives. Because they are difficult to identify, low-grade depression and social anxiety are overlooked and neglected by both the psychiatric community and society in general. What is so unfortunate is that, when diagnosed, these illnesses are easily treated.

These two disorders sabotaged any quality of life for me, and were very good at fueling my alcoholism. The only coping tool available (I thought) for my sadness and anxiety was self-medication. After my first taste of alcohol, I felt like I had finally found a solution for my sadness and fear. Soon, I became unable and unwilling to resist its intoxicating seductiveness. Because it worked so well, I quickly became dependent on its release, and continually unhappy when sober. Alcohol medicated both of my conditions so well—why on earth would I want to stop? But after a while, my rescue became my ruin. Alcohol gradually destroyed my life in every possible way.

My first attempts at recovery took place in institutions where only my alcoholism was treated. Fresh out of rehab, I was prescribed Alcoholics Anonymous meetings, because they were an effective solution for *most* alcoholics. But what nobody realized (including me) was that I was, above all else, a social phobic. Ordering a social phobic to A.A. meetings is like sending someone with a fear of heights to the Grand Canyon Skywalk, the glass-bottomed, horseshoe-shaped observation deck that extends 70 feet beyond the canyon's edge and hangs 4000 feet above the canyon floor. Twelve-step meetings where participants are expected to mingle and speak in front of a group of people are precisely the kinds of situations that social phobics fear most! I was being prescribed exactly what would send me straight back to alcohol! Consequently, when I was discharged, I always relapsed. I couldn't stay sober, because my sadness and fear were never addressed, and so I reverted to alcohol to relieve my sadness and fear. Thus began my repeated readmittance to various institutions. My relapses were buried in heaps and heaps of shame and self-disgust, further provoking me to drink with renewed vengeance, over and over again.

I had three betrothed but separate diseases to cope with, each exacerbating the other. What I call my 'triple whammy' required simultaneous treatment, and until I received medical care for all three, I was unable to recover. The first two rehabs I was admitted to treated my alcoholism without attempting to figure out *why* I drank. Dysthymia and social phobia precipitated my substance abuse, and were big reasons why I would not stop drinking, regardless of the destruction alcohol was causing in all areas of my life.

Continued use of alcohol, despite adverse consequences, baffles most people, and at the time, I couldn't understand my relapses either. I felt like a pitiful loser, disappointing my friends and family time and time again. All I knew was that I felt better when I drank. Only those who have known such fear and sadness can appreciate how I felt, and what I was willing to do to alleviate it. I was driven to do the very thing I knew was wrong, because of the extreme psychological payoffs. To me, it was a small price to pay.

There is very little compassion, sympathy, or even empathy extended by most members of society, as well as many health professionals, toward the alcoholic who repeatedly relapses after treatment. In fact, the general attitude of most people was that it was my fault—that I should just stop drinking so much.

In my *last* treatment center, and after complete detoxification from alcohol, I was fortuitously given an antidepressant. That was the breakthrough I needed to finally stay sober. I was prescribed the medication not because I was diagnosed with anxiety and depression. I was given this wonder drug because the doctor who was treating me at the time suggested that, in tough cases of alcoholism, the new generation of antidepressants *sometimes* seemed to reduce the relapse rate. Upon starting the medication, the relief I felt was overwhelmingly obvious. I could now look back and say with conviction that I had suffered from both depression and anxiety my entire life, and I could finally begin to understand what drove me to drink. I wasn't such an awful person after all!

Having experienced firsthand the 'before' and 'after' of both these primary illnesses, I could *finally* see *why* I had repeatedly experienced such stubborn and unresponsive reactions to treatments for alcoholism. Every time I stopped drinking, my depression and anxiety reared their sad and fearful heads. I had to tame them, and the only way I knew how to do that was by consuming alcohol!

In *Recovering Me, Discovering Joy*, I have documented how I could not recover until I was in remission from all three disorders, and this did not happen until I was inadvertently given a medication that simultaneously relieved all of them. When the underlying conditions were brought under control, I no longer needed to escape to feel relief. The fact that I was finally feeling good drove away any obsession and compulsion to drink.

The following pages offer a glimpse into the suffering my disease inflicted on me, my family and everybody I encountered. My life was like a semi truck barreling down some steep, narrow, winding road, impacting innocent lives all along the way. There were rocky roads ahead, and they had nothing to do with ice cream.

In this great nation of ours, alcoholism is a sad but common occurrence, costing society many valuable lives, not to mention relationships, careers and any quality of life. The devastating consequences of alcoholism and its enormous toll on the sufferer, their families and society in general are well documented. From accidental or deliberate alcohol poisoning, alcohol-related degenerative conditions and Fetal Alcohol Syndrome to drunk-driving injuries and fatalities, overcrowded jails and unemployment, it is no wonder that the direct and indirect public health costs of alcoholism are estimated to be in the hundreds of billions of dollars annually.

By sharing my story and raising awareness of low-grade chronic depression and social anxiety disorder, my hope is to impact the incidence of substance abuse and its relapse rate in the world today. It is my mission to bring about a better understanding of the strong correlation between these three profound dysfunctions. If my story encourages better screening for depression and anxiety, or possibly saves one person the frustration I endured, then this book will have served its intended purpose.

Today I'm enjoying my journey. I am at peace with God and my fellow human beings. I am leading the best life I have ever had and today, I feel the way I deserved to feel since the day I was born. I love my position in the universe, and I want others to take advantage of my discoveries and the enlightenment gleaned from my daily recoveries.

Recovering Me, Discovering Joy is about the successes that I enjoy today in every area of my life. Faced with the likelihood of permanent insanity, or even death, I somehow found my way back. From the gift of desperation, I unearthed a survival kit of tools for daily living, and gained a positive perspective on life. But I had to hit bottom and surrender my will to God to fully appreciate what recovery had in store for me. And it was only then that I found this glorious way to live.

Recovering Me, Discovering Joy is a collection of insights, some selected from books written a long time ago, others taken from sources more contemporary. These profundities are reiterated (for some cannot be mentioned often enough), and told in a different way, by someone who has suffered, but is a victor, not a victim.

There are musings and stories from my life (some humorous, others anything but). Along with my experiences, I've included quotes from people at the top of their field, passages from the Bible, and concepts learned from the 12-step recovery program.

The wisdom that grows from adversity can be profound, but to be effective, these ideas must be understood, accepted and utilized to the point of subconscious, involuntary action. Wisdom is like data that has been entered into a computer. It is only effective if it is downloaded and implemented. Implementation is the key. All those little daily meditation books that are so popular these days suggest the importance of ongoing reminders. Similarly, this book is meant to be returned to, and to serve as a reference when reevaluating our progress in all dimensions of our life.

My intent has been to record some of the life-enhancing ideas that I have discovered during my years in recovery from my 'triple whammy,' and I have found that retelling my experiences keeps me humble, and the lessons learned 'green.' I've also learned that what is discovered and not shared is lost. The negativity and destructiveness in my life has vanished. God willing, the positive effect of my recovery will have a beneficial effect on everyone that I and others come in contact with, impacting generations to come.

It is never too late to recognize good principles, to begin to live by them, and reap the benefits as you surely will. I've faced life from the side of fear and the side of faith, and want to encourage you to bridge the great divide in order to achieve your full potential, and to find contentment. Like it or not, we are all on this same grand highway called life. We must all deal with life's inevitable physical and psychological setbacks, but take heart—joy will return to each and every one of us if we are open to it and willing to accept it.

It is my sincere hope that this book serves as a life-transforming event for all who read it, and that your journey is a beautiful one, as you continue to recover from life's daily challenges. May *Recovering Me, Discovering Joy* be of some help, comfort and inspiration to you as you learn to become the child of God you were born to be. From tragedy can come magnificent compensation. I am living proof of that. So, be sure and wait for that precious moment when you finally realize that everything you've been through is worth it.

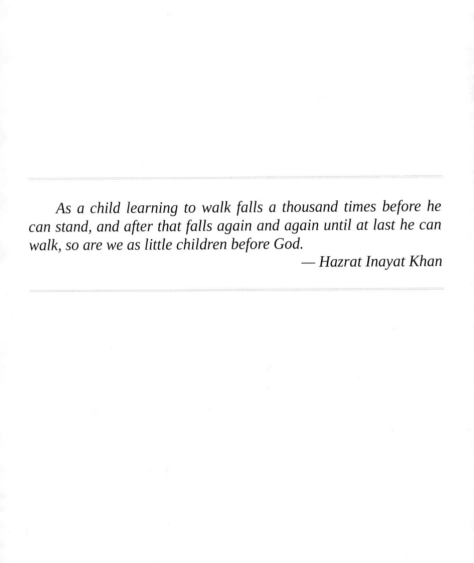

As a child learning to walk falls a thousand times before he can stand, and after that falls again and again until at last he can walk, so are we as little children before God.

— Hazrat Inayat Khan

Recovering Me
Discovering Joy

Part One

Recovering Me

Naked, Wet and Hungry

Someone once said, "We are born naked, wet and hungry, get slapped on our backside...and then we crawl through hostile territory..." This is a bleak way of saying that we can all expect trouble in our lives, for in this world there will always be pain—the innocent are not exempt.

The diamond cannot be polished without friction, nor man perfected without trials.

— Confucius

Difficulties are necessary and essential for growth. The phrase 'personal growth' is tossed around all the time, but what exactly is it? It is the mental, spiritual, and emotional process by which we move from self-limitation, deterioration and failure to self-improvement and victorious living.

Many of us would not bother to really learn a lesson well unless driven to do so by sorrow, failure, or illness. On the flip side, not all suffering instructs. If that were true, we would all be very wise. But in suffering lies the *opportunity* for instruction, and for growth.

When tough problems are regarded as fertile soil for opportunity, they become inherently good, not inherently bad. By interpreting them as useful, we are better able to attack them with a positive attitude. As we learn to capitalize on hardships, they stop working against us, become less threatening, and start working for us. They don't need to destroy us, or even negatively impact us—ever!

Some of the ways we grow from times of trouble are: we develop a greater appreciation of life, our spiritual beliefs deepen, we feel stronger and more effective, we grow closer to others; and finally, unexpected paths sometimes appear.

Weapons of Mass Instruction

That's what problems are. Without problems, there would be no progress. Fire wasn't discovered until man was confronted with the problem of staying warm. Cures for diseases are usually not found until enough people have been stricken to make discovering treatments a top priority.

A life filled with vicissitudes, uncertainty and hard lessons provides us with skills to better approach new challenges that come along. Having said that, it makes sense that we might consider ourselves fortunate when disappointments come sooner rather than later in life. We learn early on how to start over again, how not to be afraid, and how to appreciate each situation's benefits, so when that inevitable life-defining obstacle appears before us *again*, we'll have the courage and the know-how to continue moving forward.

The first and most important step in problem solving is recognizing that we have one. We can't solve a problem unless we can identify it for what it is, no matter how challenging it may seem. After recognizing and accepting a challenge, we need to adjust our attitude and thought process to reflect the new direction we must take.

Let's take, for example, the common problem of clutter. Most of us in the United States need to stay on top of this on a daily basis, or we would soon be up to our eyeballs in newspapers and other accumulated things. We could ignore this problem, making it worse; we could begrudgingly pick up, organize and store our stuff, making us feel worse; or we can look at the problem for its potential, and decide that the modern day problem of clutter is really only about great ways to store stuff. That's how easy it is to bring problems over to our side.

Problems come in all sizes. The problem of clutter is nothing compared to what my husband had to endure. Bill suffered a brain hemorrhage, paralyzing the right side of his body. This massive stroke came with very little warning, and left him devastatingly changed. After it was determined that he wasn't going to die (thank God!), the problem of recovery had to be analyzed, and priorities set. His doctors needed to assess the damage to his body. What problem was most urgent? Learning to drink, eat and swallow food again were the top priorities.

Over time, and after some clarity of thought returned, Bill took it upon himself to start more extensive physical therapy. The use of his right hand was critical to him, so he concentrated on regaining the use of that hand as his next priority. Bill's the first to admit that he couldn't dance before his stroke, so while it might have been of great concern had he been Michael Flatley, from *Lord of the Dance*, learning to dance wasn't an issue.

The most important thing Bill had going for him after he suffered his stroke was that he was motivated. He wanted to get better. He wanted to recover. He was under a tremendous amount of stress, and had a rotten attitude in the beginning, but gradually came to realize how nonproductive that was.

Now, a certain amount of stress is necessary in order for us to grow and thrive. Just as the tension of the wind against the sail causes the sailboat to move, so stress is necessary for us to progress through life. Continuing the same metaphor, did you ever wonder how the same wind can drive two boats in completely opposite directions? Or how similar events in our lives can drive one person forward and the other backward? The storms of life can lift us to magnificent glory, or drive us to incomprehensible demoralization. Where we end up depends on the condition of our physical, spiritual, emotional and mental sails. Stress is not about the event itself, but about our response to it. And our reaction to a situation depends on our perception of the event, and on our connection with God.

A good example of this is the common roller-coaster ride. Some people pay a lot of money searching for the ultimate thrill ride. Whole vacations are planned around finding the biggest, fastest, steepest, scariest rides. Some people enjoy being pushed to their limits, and laugh at their jumpy stomachs. Other people are horrified of roller-coasters. Their reaction to the experience is *distress*. It's the same ride, but our mental and physical responses determine whether or not it will be stressful or enjoyable. Therefore, when we become 'stressed,' it's not because of our outward circumstance. It's because of our reaction to it.

Are You a Grape or a Marble?

When discussing stress, I like to use the example of the ordinary vice grip that many men keep attached to the workbench in their garage for special projects that require grabbing hold of and securing various objects. Let's press two things that aren't usually associated with this grip. First, squeeze a marble in it, and then squeeze a grape. Which one does better under pressure? If we place the marble under enough pressure, it will crack, crumble and fall apart. Because it is hardened, and not flexible, it will shatter. Such is the case with an angry, unforgiving, or bitter heart.

Now, let's apply the same amount of pressure to the grape. What happens? Sure the grape won't look the same but something beneficial is gleaned. There is a positive outcome. Grape juice— the sweet substance of life. Life-sustaining nourishment is produced.

How will we react when life puts 'the squeeze on?' It all depends on the condition of our insides, the attitude of our heart, and our relationship with God. If we are made of good stuff, challenges won't break us, but will change us for the better.

Life is a series of problems. Either we're in one now, we're just coming out of one, or we're getting ready to go into another one. The reason for this is that God is more interested in our character than our comfort. He is more interested in making our life holy than He is in making our life easy. But the great news is that He is there to help us every step of the way. God is bigger than all our problems combined!

One way to keep from becoming bitter or broken is to look at the lighter side of situations. Laughter is a powerful reliever of stress, and can be a great healer. When we laugh, we exercise our abdominal muscles. The blood flow increases throughout our bodies. Doctors who have done studies on the effectiveness of laughter look at it as the equivalent of jogging on the inside. That's how effective it can be, and it's so much fun.

Through humor, we take hold of life with a playful, creative and not so somber manner. It temporarily relieves us of life's daily pressures. Humor is a positive approach to life's troubles, and helps us transcend them. Sometimes, it even pulls us away from the problem long enough to see a possible solution. Today, very few days go by without Bill and me enjoying a big hearty, gut-jiggling laugh, either at ourselves, or at our little world around us.

Finding Value in Our Valleys

In *The Ways We Choose*, Dave Carey, a prisoner of war in Hanoi for 5½ years during the '60s and a good friend of mine, talks a lot about what kept the prisoners going, and what coping skills they used during their time of extreme adversity. Isolated in a tiny cell, tied up, repeatedly beaten within inches of his life, in excruciating pain, and given little more than rice and water to eat and drink for years, you would think that, now, Dave would be bitter, yet today, Dave is a shining example of how much good can come from severe and gut-wrenching circumstances.

Dave suggests that three of the reasons for their success in surviving such a harsh environment were that they chose to grow through the experience, they kept their sense of humor and they kept the faith, which gave them hope. Humor, more so than any other human attribute, offers us the ability to rise above any situation.

Laughter was the way they coped with the pressure. Laughter was the way they kept their sanity, and held everything together. It was the way they let off steam, keeping things in perspective and maintaining their balance. Dave's stories of the tricks they played on the guards are hilarious. The prisoners made their captors look like idiots at times, solely for each other's entertainment.

One of Dave's fellow inmate's families owned a farm in Kansas and a long running joke began when one of the guards asked him what his family grew. He told him that they produced 'updoc.' The captor proceeded to go around asking the rest of the prisoners, "What's up doc?" leaving the Americans laughing with each other whenever they could. The joke continued to evolve into entire conversations about 'updoc.' At one point, the guard even learned the recipe for 'updoc' bread.

He and his cellmates *chose* to make a determined effort to learn and grow, even in captivity. Instead of vegetating, they were driven to emerge from the prisons better than when they were shot down. He spent a great deal of time alone in jail, but at irregular intervals the prisoners were moved from prison to prison and from cell to cell. This gave them opportunities to live with different men, and enrich their impoverished existence.They used a lot of ingenuity to survive. When they were apart, they used elaborate ways of communicating.

Dave learned to play the piano in prison from another fellow inmate who had taken piano lessons as a child. No, they didn't happen to have a piano in their cells. So how do you learn to play the piano without a piano, you may be wondering? They took some toilet paper and glued it together with rice, and then used ashes and dirt to draw a keyboard on it. Using this, Dave learned to read the keyboard and sheet music. He even practiced all the little finger exercises that piano students use. He practiced faithfully, and on Sundays he gave concerts for his fellow prisoners, spreading out his piano at the end of his cell.

Dave also learned to type in prison, using a similar process. He learned the keyboard first—A, S, D, F, G, etc. Then he folded his blanket so that it sloped on one side, pulled a white thread out of the border, and sewed it onto the slanted portion in big stitches, with a stitch where each typewriter key should be. Using this 'typewriter,' he typed his memoirs, and letters to everybody he knew. The men also took French classes, formal speech classes, and even formed the Hanoi chapter of Toastmasters.

Adversity has the effect of eliciting talents which in prosperous circumstances would have lain dormant.

— Horace

In times of reversal, if we look for the lessons or the hidden blessings, the ordeal will seem less traumatic. We at least see a reason for our pain. What we glean from a setback will bring solace and compensation for any suffering. Besides, great things come not from happy, contented times, but from struggling, searching times. Once we get through difficult times, most of us (if we recognize the lessons involved) can look back and say either "That wasn't so bad," or better yet, "It was the best thing that *ever* happened to me."

My husband, Bill, suffered from an illness much different to mine, but we came together and rallied. We fought for our lives side by side, and together learned a lot about recovery. Today, Bill and I have a much better relationship than we ever had before his stroke and all of my struggles. In retrospect, our challenges turned out to be necessary for advancement, as opposed to what we thought at the time was misfortune.

Today, because I've hit a few rough patches already, when I hit a snag, I bring out my survival tool kit and try to recall earlier lessons. In recovery, the quantity of problems that I face everyday has been significantly reduced, and the efficiency with which I handle the ones I have has greatly improved. The problems I have today aren't as terrifying. They are more positive, service-oriented problems. "How can I best help this person out?" "Should I let go in a certain area regarding my children?"

But, like a hawk on a bunny, I know that some day in the future an incomprehensible setback will descend, once again changing the landscape of my life forever. There will be other losses, and other casualties to mourn. I will be chosen again to take what I can from whatever comes my way.

Life is Tough—but We are Tougher

Painful events will happen; it's our responsibility to put them behind us. We must remember that, within each difficulty, the seed for its solution is stored, and quite possibly the seed of greatness is there, too, just waiting to be found. We can choose to either go to work for a rich harvest, or wallow in our suffering. The choice is ours.

Today, we can have a large reservoir of courage and hope that, whatever happens, everything will be all right. When afflictions of the body, mind and soul come crashing down upon us, our dilemma must be—how can I add value to this situation?

Well, enough generalizing about problems and solutions. Let me now tell you about what happened to me...

Recovery as a Unique Advantage

Someone once said that from the day we are born, we are in a continual state of recovery. At any given time, there is some part of us recovering. I never thought about being in perpetual recovery until, for a period of time, I met with a counselor.

With my life in freefall, it was highly recommended that I get help, and I wanted to appease certain individuals near and dear to me, so in a somewhat defiant, borderline-resentful state, I plopped my recovery-reluctant body in Ms. Counselor's office, hoping to sweet-talk her into believing that my life was just ducky, that I was hip, slick and cool, and that I certainly didn't need *her* help. My strategy was to 'flip the script,' and so I started by asking her about herself. Curious enough, she went along with me for a while, and we talked about various ailments and recovery from them. Somewhere in our clever repartee, I heard her say, "I recover every day."

Aha! So she had problems, too! I don't recall anything else about my session with her, but I remember that.

We are all in recovery, to some degree, on a daily basis. The day we are born, we begin to recover from the birthing process. Every night, our bodies recover from the day's work. Some of us are recovering from bigger things, but I think you get my point.

Recovery to a Better Normal

One of the hallmarks of being human is the ability to overcome trauma. Webster's Dictionary defines the word 'recover' this way: to get back, regain; to bring back to normal position or condition. But while we're recovering, why not use this special time in our lives and the momentum of recovery to further better ourselves —to shoot for a *better* normal?

When we find ourselves recovering from a stroke, heart attack, depression, or a death in the family, rather than just getting back to our former situation, why not use this time to our advantage? Recovery can be an extremely useful time in our lives. It can help propel us to far greater heights than we ever dreamed imaginable.

After 9/11, our nation suffered great sadness and terrible heartache. But through our grief we knew somehow the tragedy would make us better. It became an opportunity for transformation from normal, to an *improved* normal. Now because of 9/11 our airports are safer, our airplanes have been reconfigured, our borders are more secure. And we continue to enhance our safety every day. Healing is hard work, but with it, wisdom emerges. And, one of the best things about recovery is that it's limitless!

My husband, Bill had a big recovery on his hands after suffering a massive stroke at the peak of his career in the medical device business. At the time, he was only 52. He was a good tennis player, a runner, and coached our son's baseball team in his spare time. After his stroke, there was still plenty of hope, but for a long time, his eyes couldn't see any. They were still focused on the doors that were closing.

Bill had to grieve multiple losses, and even after this untimely catastrophic event, I don't think he had reached the lowest point of his life until finally, he hit *bottom* when he fell and cracked his ribs while working in his office one day.

After he fell, he spent the afternoon on the floor crying out to God. During that time, Bill realized that God would do for him what he could not alone. When he finally bottomed out, he was in a much better position to look for the potential in his setback, but he had to let God show him the way.

How do we know when we've hit bottom? We will know, because we will *want* to change, we will *want* recovery, we will *want* to surrender, we will *want* to do whatever is required to get better. Before hitting bottom, we don't *really* want to turn things over. We still want to be in control, and we don't like to give that up unless it's absolutely necessary. We would rather remain the same because, at the time, it *seems easier.*

The Gift of Desperation

This may seem counterintuitive, but 'bottoms' provide many benefits. They give us a chance to stop our free fall, to change direction. At the lowest level of any predicament, there is only one direction out, and that is up. 'Bottoms' usually provide us with a time out, a space in time to look at possible solutions. They can be devastating enough that we are temporarily relieved from the daily pressures of life. At my 'bottom,' the only hope I had was that things would ultimately get better, and I clung to that.

'Bottoms' give us the gift of desperation. Yes, I said a gift— that critical dissatisfaction with ourselves and our circumstances which we need in order to take a good hard look at our predicament, and our part in it. 'Bottoms' supply us with a sense of urgency. During this painful time, we are forced to take a look at ourselves, which is the necessary first step toward self-awareness and self-correction.

A feeling of guilt is often times essential. It can motivate us to change. 'Bottoms' humble us, making us teachable again. In essence, they are ideal human learning environments, for it is sometimes only when the road grows narrow that we ever take the time to consider our soul, our God, or even our life's work.

Another benefit from the valleys in our lives is that they can provide a foundation for a profound spiritual experience. They can be excellent opportunities for spiritual growth, guiding us toward new and better directions. A setback can be a golden opportunity for us to really take care of 'self' and gain a new perspective as to where God is leading us.

Despite the negativity associated with 'bottoms,' I am grateful for mine. My 'bottom' taught me an excellent lesson in *humility.* I wasn't interested in finding a better way to live until alcohol beat me to within inches of my life. Everybody's 'bottom' is different, and that was mine. It wasn't until then that I asked myself whether maybe my way of doing things wasn't so great, after all. I had to decide that I wanted recovery, that I had to have it, and this epiphany only came after I was physically, emotionally, mentally, and spiritually bankrupt. I had to bottom out in every area of my life.

The unholy trinity—me, myself and I—had gotten me into a whole bunch of trouble. It took a divine two-by-four to get me to realize that maybe my will needed to be realigned to better fit His. I didn't see where this new way of living was going to help, but I had exhausted all my options.

If I was ever going to love and take care of myself, I had to first take an honest look at what I had become, and then start to work on my character defects. I had to figure out what I was responsible for, and what was not my responsibility. At the same time, I had to recognize the people, places and things that were beyond my control, and accept that I was powerless over them.

The 12 Steps as a Template for Living

One of the glorious things about recovery is that finding help is easy. In the United States today, there are tremendous resources available to help facilitate any type of rehabilitation process. One good resource is the basic spiritual laws of recovery. They are explained and simplified by what is now widely known as the 12-step Program of Recovery, which originated in Alcoholics Anonymous.

After years of A.A. getting and keeping thousands of alcoholics sober, the idea finally came about that if these principles worked so well for drunks, why couldn't similar standards benefit other areas of society as well? After all, the alcoholic or addict (recovering and otherwise) does not have a lock on insanity, or a monopoly on human suffering and unhappiness.

Because of the success of the Alcoholics Anonymous program, many other twelve-step programs for other behavioral problems have been modeled after it. This twelve-step program way of living has helped people over and over again, not only to rediscover themselves, but to learn to be assets to their loved ones, and society in general. For this reason, the ideas of the twelve-step program have gradually come into greater favor and wider acceptance.

Twelve-step programs (of which there are now over 200) focus on three different areas. First, they acknowledge that our basic human resources, such as intelligence and knowledge, are not enough for us to solve all of our problems. Second, they focus on our need to let God guide our actions and thoughts. Third, they suggest ways that God can be brought into our daily life so that we can live the best possible life that we can.

The spiritual 12-step recovery program, when fleshed out, is about love and service. As a universal template for living a better life, it's a wonderful tool. It simplifies and enumerates the steps we need to take in order to heal. Let me tell you, when I was first exposed to this simple program, I was so far gone that for all I knew the 12 steps could have been the divine secrets of some sort of coed Ya-Ya Sisterhood. But after years of following them, 'the steps' are no longer an enigma to me. I try to follow the 12-step course in all areas of my life today.

Those of us in recovery are grateful that we have been given the spiritual 12-step programs to help guide us. These steps support us, and encourage us to respond properly, regardless of our predicament.

Successful recovery can transport us from the depths of despair to enormous peace and serenity. It did for Bill, and it did for me. Having surrendered and accepted a new and better way to live, I have my trust and faith in God that I am at this very moment exactly where I am meant to be. I am joyfully living according to His plan, and encourage others to do the same.

Dysthymia—
A Neglected Disorder

Everybody is depressed occasionally, and to a certain degree this emotion can be beneficial. Feeling blue can help motivate us to seek a solution to the problem that is weighing us down. Depression is a normal experience, and more often than not it is triggered by a negative life event, but sometimes depression becomes so intense or prolonged that it causes harmful, even life-threatening behavior.

Depression, in its various forms, affects nearly 19 million Americans each year according to the National Institute of Mental Health (NIMH). With prolonged major depression, shortages or imbalances of mood-influencing chemicals in the brain usually play a role.

Studies show that depressive illness can and often does run in families. The genetic connection is beyond controversy. Another proven fact is that women, as a group, are twice as likely to experience depression.

Up until the age of 46, I had gone through my entire life feeling blue, never feeling quite right. I was missing a dimension, a dimension of joy. I don't remember ever experiencing real happiness until I was successfully in recovery from alcoholism. By then, I was already in my mid-forties. My life had looked all right, but my *quality* of life was severely compromised by my low-grade blue moods.

There was rarely any reason for my dark moods, but they transcended everything I did. My internal outlook diminished all peak experiences. I envied other people's rosy perspectives, and often wondered how they could feel so good. I felt deprived. I felt like I was missing out on something very basic.

There was a sad undertone lurking beneath even my happiest events. I'd wake up not really wanting to get out of bed. I could never quite shake the awful, all-encompassing feeling of "What was the use of it all?" At times, I merely went through the motions of living. I remember thinking that everybody couldn't feel like this, or it would be the topic of conversation on the news, talk shows and amongst my friends. I don't know how many times I asked myself, "Am I the only person who feels like this?" Somehow, I knew that I couldn't be the only person who felt so low.

Because I usually put on a happy face, nobody seemed aware or showed concern that I had this constant drag pulling me down. I subconsciously thought that if I acted normal, I might feel normal. I knew something was wrong, but I felt that I couldn't describe it to anybody without them telling me to just get over it. I do remember my husband giving me pep talks from time to time, but the way I felt just wasn't pronounced enough to seek professional help, or so I thought.

I figured I was different, but I didn't know what to do about it. I didn't think there was anything legitimate that could ever relieve my cheerlessness. I always thought psychiatry was for crazy people, and the only way to feel better was to pick myself up by my bootstraps and do something on my own to alleviate my sadness.

The best I ever hoped to feel occurred when I was totally distracted, immersed in something that diverted my attention or completely consumed me. So, I worked hard at staying busy, achieving and excelling in whatever I did, in spite of the way I felt.

I now know that all those years I was suffering from chronic, low-grade depression. This condition, called dysthymic disorder, is a long-term, less severe form of depression that is rarely detected, recognized or talked about.

I Hated the Way I Felt

I spent the majority of my waking hours battling a constant smothering, confining hopelessness, until my depression manifested itself in a more outwardly visible debilitating condition. Then, it wasn't until I received therapy for what my psychiatrist believed to be *reactive depression* caused by my alcoholism that my dysthymia was alleviated.

Some psychiatrists and substance abuse counselors recognize or diagnose *reactive depression* in their patients. Believing their patient's depression to be a secondary depression due to the social complications of alcoholism or other addictions, these professionals give them an anti-depressant in order to provide relief. And so they did for me. When I was given an anti-depressant, I began to feel good for the first time in my life. For me, it was a life-changing event.

Why hadn't I recognized that I had a treatable disorder sooner? Besides, how could I say that I wasn't happy when I didn't know what happy was? And sure enough, when researching this mood disorder, I found that the majority of people suffering from depression don't understand what they are experiencing. With most people, clinical depression goes unnoticed and untreated.

I never knew there was such a thing as chronic low-grade depression, but I was far from alone in not recognizing my depression for what it was. According to NIMH, only 20% of people with mild depression recognize what it is and seek help, and only 50% of people with severe, incapacitating depression ever receive medical advice.

There are a number of reasons why many people are reluctant to seek professional help. In this great nation of ours, there *still* exists a general feeling that seeing a psychiatrist represents some sort of personal failure. A psychiatric problem is no more a personal failure than diabetes or heart disease, but we don't want to be classified as 'abnormal.' We truly want to believe that everything is 'fine,' but no problem has ever been solved by denial.

Because I hadn't experienced any of the more blatant manifestations of depression such as insomnia, loss of appetite, or even thoughts of suicide, I had decided that what I felt couldn't be depression, and that I was just not as happy as most people. I was able to function, but I felt bad much more often than I felt good (instead of the other way around—the way most people feel).

At times, getting through my daily life was difficult for me, but I always talked myself out of having a serious condition. With few outward manifestations, chronic low-grade depression doesn't always escalate into a crisis (thank God it did for me), therefore it seems as though there is nothing to address. It is an insidious disease in that it exists, but nobody knows about it other than the sufferer. You feel terrible but, essentially, it's a non-issue.

The bottom line is that if the depression doesn't result in some other more blatant negative condition, such as substance abuse, many of us are likely to suffer our entire lives. When I was *finally* given an anti-depressant, I felt like an incredible weight had been lifted, one that I had been carrying all of my life. For me, it was serendipitous, but most medical doctors working in alcohol treatment centers believe that if an alcoholic stops drinking and goes to Alcoholics Anonymous meetings, his alcoholism and other problems will disappear. More often than not, one can explain failures in treatment programs as related to the failure to diagnose and treat other illnesses, such as depression or anxiety disorders. Fortunately these attitudes and oversights are improving, but not fast enough.

In my case and I'm sure in the cases of others, A.A. couldn't solve the issues that fueled my alcoholism. If I still felt bad, how could I not want to feel good (i.e., drink)? Alcoholism was merely the pimple on the elephant. How could my alcoholism be treated effectively if the provoking factors raged on? Raising awareness among substance abuse professionals about some sort of screening, diagnosis and/or intervention for dysthymia and social phobia could quite possibly reduce the relapse rate among addicts and alcoholics. By implementing better screening tools, they could quite possibly impact the huge nationwide problem of substance abuse and its societal consequences.

Two signs of chronic low-grade depression that I am now aware of are: a depressed mood that doesn't pass, and difficulty getting motivated to do the things we normally enjoy. I suffered from both of these, and nothing alleviated my dark thoughts until alcohol was introduced into my life. The change in the way I felt was some sort of miracle, I was sure. I was astonished that I finally felt good. I noticed that when I had a glass of wine, I felt better *immediately*. This liquid elixir offered such great relief that I looked forward to the next opportunity to partake. Since alcohol was my only avenue (albeit a false one) to a sense of well-being, soon the avoidance of my God-awful desperation became the compass that guided me. I sought its assistance again and again, and over time my *self-medication* developed into dependence, but as far as I was concerned, the relief I felt far outweighed any derogatory effects.

Death by Her own Hand

The consequences of untreated depression can be tragic. I share this intimate portrait of my Mom's struggles in the hope that it can help someone in some way. I tell her story not for sympathy, but to show the impact depression/suicide can have on a family. She had struggled with depression her entire life, and when a number of major life-losses made living unbearable, her chronic low-grade depression escalated, and she turned to suicide.

My Mom worked hard every day, and was an excellent homemaker. She baked, cleaned and sewed, and with four children, she had plenty to keep her busy. Her kids came first, Dad second, and she always put herself last. She was a good wife and mother, and was always there for her children.

Sometime in our teenage years, Mom became lethargic, and began taking to her bed more and more. Something strange was happening, but none of us could pinpoint it.

My siblings' and my teenage years were lived during that tumultuous decade of the sixties. My brothers, Fred and Wayne, and sister Eileen and I were caught up in our own lives, and for many reasons, we didn't much notice that Mom was changing. Her fierce motivation was diminishing. All the signs of melancholia were there. She had even asked for sleeping pills, complaining of insomnia. Caught up in our own self-centered teenage years, none of us ever imagined she was contemplating suicide. Her depression intensified after she was diagnosed with colitis. Most mentally sound people can deal with a diagnosis such as this. They might develop a short-term depression, but then they move on to acceptance. Mom never did. Her kids (her life) were at various difficult stages of adolescence, and Mom was now suffering from an incurable disease which, in her mind, would bankrupt the family. Evidently, she thought her illness would be too great a financial and emotional burden on us. All of this turned out to be a lethal combination of setbacks. My mother's situation was devastating enough in that she could no longer endure the pain of it, and so she chose death as a solution. I truly believe she thought she was doing us a favor.

She took her own life for a number of irrational reasons, one of which was to escape the torment of depression. The pain of suicidal depression like this is unimaginable to most people, although to a certain degree, I can relate to how she must have felt. To her, the unknown was far less terrifying than the unbearable frustration, futility, and hopelessness of her daily life.

One September day, when orange, red and mustard-colored leaves graced the big Midwest trees, we laid her to rest in the dark and tender earth forever. We clothed her in her one good dress. It was pale blue, and had she not chosen death, she might have worn it to my wedding—or sewed up a new one, had things been different.

She lived vicariously, through and for her children, but in the process, she sold herself short. One of her big mistakes was that she spent her entire life living for others, never leaving any time to take care of herself. She couldn't have known that her ultimate self-sacrifice would leave a trail of devastation in its wake.

In some ways, my Dad, my siblings and I were blessed. The procession of official encounters that can compound a grieving family's suffering never materialized. My brothers, Fred and Wayne, were questioned, since they were at home at the time, but Mom had left a note and other evidence which kept us from spending hours at the police station and the degradation of being treated as suspects in something untoward. The question of homicide never took shape, and our innocence was never shattered by a tough investigation.

According to Wayne, she had sent him out to rake the leaves. He thought this was odd since there were very few on the ground at the time. Fred, who was sleeping, as he was working the night shift at a local General Motors plant, was woken by the sound of a gunshot and found Mom's body lying on the bathroom floor. He also found her note, which he related to us later. I was angered that the police had confiscated her letter, which was meant for us. I was mad because she hadn't left us much, and now I was being denied the last thing she had touched. I wanted her last words.

Her death was a terrible loss, but somehow we muddled through the first few days afterwards. Neighbors sent cards and flowers, and brought prepared food, along with their condolences, and one of Mom's sisters came to stay with us. Dad was strong, and suffered in silence, but I know he was deeply hurt and traumatized.

After a while, a sorrowful routine descended upon our weakened household. Eileen and I took turns with the laundry. Dad's shirts had to be cleaned and pressed for his work the next day, and for meals, we came up with simple recipes we remembered from watching and helping Mom. I battled anger and despair, but looking back, this period of my life would not be my worst.

Secretly, I took solace in the tears I shared with my sister. Eventually, the sharp pain of loss became a dull pain, but I was flat —any small amount of magic that life had to offer was now gone. After Mom died, I continued to suffer deep insecurity and low self-worth long after the acute grieving stage had passed.

Some people say that you only lose someone when you quit remembering them. If that's the case, I'll never be deprived of her.

My mother suffered from both depression and social phobia (see the chapter on this later), without the benefit of today's therapies. She was a terrific person, with mental disorders that are treatable today. After a while, I understood to a certain degree, and identified with her, and her situation has helped me to grapple with my own inner demons.

Soon, after Mom died, I met my husband, Bill, who could make me laugh, and always get me out of my doldrums. I also had the weekends to look forward to, with cocktails which would lift me from despair, if only for a short time, so I was okay for a while, just being able to anticipate these brief periods of relief.

Later, with a successful husband and two beautiful children, people started telling me that I 'had it made.' I looked around me, and had to believe them. Outside appearances made it seem so, but even in the best of situations possible, I still wasn't happy. How could that be? I felt like an ingrate—unappreciative, and feeling this way only added to my misery. I couldn't see a future for myself that offered promise or purpose. My low mood wasn't related to any circumstances in my life. No matter what happened, depression remained my default state, the place to which my mind always reverted. Despite being a successful woman, wife and mother, I was despondent. It just didn't make sense. And the last thing I wanted to be was a despicable, self-involved whiner!

After my kids started school, I tried various volunteer projects, but nothing seemed to really capture my interest. I should have recognized my situation as merely a plateau, a resting place where I could decide what I wanted to do next. What I failed to do was come up with new dreams. Like many people, I required total involvement in living, working and winning to feel good, but it was difficult to do when I was depressed, and masking my feelings with alcohol.

My incentive, drive and motivation (the very things that were sometimes the only avenues out of my despair) gradually deteriorated and slipped away. The possibility of experiencing the thrill and excitement of achievement vanished. Like taking a beautifully colored lithograph and draining all the color from it, my mind sab-otaged any joy, every time.

There were still bigger and better things to experience, I just hadn't discovered them yet. My depressed state of mind kept me from seeing a way out. I was totally unaware that the way I felt could lead to other difficulties and affect many other people, espe-cially those close to me. Effective therapy for my depression might have kept me from alcohol dependence, and saved me and my fam-ily years of dysfunction.

Instead, I covered my feelings up—I drowned them. I went through the motions of living, but I was just a shell of the person I had been, or could become. I was slowly becoming addicted to al-cohol, requiring more and more to get the same affect. It had thrust its powerful hooks into me.

Habits are at First Cobwebs, then Cables

Over a period of years, this escape mechanism from my un-happiness became the friend whose comfort I sought on a regular basis. I didn't realize at the time that, since alcohol is a depressant, I was fueling my dysthymia. All the time, I thought I was suppress-ing it. Eventually, I became caught in the vortex of addiction, pow-erless to stop or even slow down. My descent into alcoholism ate away at me, and all my relationships were on the brink of destruc-tion. Whenever I stopped drinking, I would relapse into depression. It was a vicious cycle. But at the same time, I couldn't understand why staying sober was so difficult for me.

When an alcoholic or drug addict does not recover after being in a treatment center, the attitude of the facility, the employer, the family, and the world is that it is the patient's fault. For this very reason, every time I relapsed, I felt extreme humiliation, shame, emptiness and disgrace.

In one of the last recovery centers in which I had the privilege to be treated, antidepressants were prescribed for some of us. Some health-care professionals recommend antidepressants for their newly sober patients. Many of us are depressed when we first get sober. After all, we've created a lot of wreckage, and now have to begin to clean everything up! When I was given an antidepressant, I was unwittingly and serendipitously given treatment for the scourges of my existence (my low-grade depression and social anxiety). Amazingly, I began to feel better, and didn't need to revert to alcohol to get through my days.

After people in recovery begin to feel better, some ask to be taken off the medication, since there can be negative side effects. These same people go on to do well without medication, for drug therapy was just needed to get them past their initial situational (and understandable) depression. That wasn't the case for me. Since I was finally feeling good, I was terrified by the notion of going off my medication.

The group of antidepressants known as selective serotonin reuptake inhibitors (SSRIs), such as Paxil or Prozac, have worked like a miracle in conquering my lifelong battle with chronic low-grade depression. Quitting my meds is no longer an option—I know, because I tried to quit at one point in time.

I had been off Prozac for over a month (after slowly weaning myself), and was sitting in my office with Bill on a spectacular, sunny, quintessential San Diego day. I hadn't a care in the world, but suddenly all my thoughts began to turn to gloom and doom, and then I burst out crying. I went back on an antidepressant, and have felt good ever since.

Get Help!

Today, I feel as though I have been given 'wings' to rise above the difficulties inherent in my Mom's situation. For me, I am delighted to say that depression and anxiety have been eliminated from my life by this new generation of antidepressants.

I now realize that I am a critical link between the past and the future. I am in the prime position to either corrupt or correct this chain. Instead of allowing depression, anxiety and quite possibly substance abuse to trickle down through the generations, I can change the course of many lives by sharing what I've learned.

In recovery, not only am I blessed with extraordinary relationships, but I also have a clearer concept of the possibilities that lie before me. I now know that it is important for anybody with recurrent and serious depression to get help as soon as possible, in order to prevent the accumulative effect, not only on those of us who suffer, but on everybody around us. For those of us already receiving treatment, it's a terrible mistake to discontinue the therapy without first discussing it with our doctor. For me, medication saved my life, and has led to a freedom from depression I never thought possible.

Studies show that taking care of ourselves helps defend against depression. Regular exercise, a well-balanced diet, and a faith in a higher power are good habits that help to ward off this debilitating illness. Religion can provide hope, direction and comfort to those of us who feel lost. But when none of these help, there are multiple therapies available, and numerous professionals who can help. Statistics show that more than 80% of people with depression improve when they are given appropriate treatment. Recent advances in the treatment of depression have helped millions, and saved many lives.

Both scientific and psychotherapeutic evidence point to a general feeling of mental and emotional well-being as our natural emotional state as we go through life. We all deserve to feel good, but sometimes this doesn't happen without help. Since there are treatments available today for most mental or emotional suffering we may encounter, we must never give in to depression, nor accept it as the norm.

FEAR—Face Everything And Recover

In our ongoing attempts to demystify this basic human instinct, much has been written about fear. It is just a normal human emotion, but because it influences how we are going to respond to situations, it is important to understand the nature of fear.

Fear is not a bad feeling, and can even be a great motivator, but we must first recognize and acknowledge our fears before we can make them work for us. When we are born, we are only born with two fears—fear of loud noises, and fear of falling. The rest are learned, and therefore we can 'unlearn' the ones that are unnecessary for our well-being.

As with other emotions, there are healthy levels of fear, and not so healthy levels. Reacting to fear in a negative manner (i.e., making wrong choices) can be a huge obstacle to our growth, where we want to go, or who we want to become. Sometimes, the only difference between success and failure is our response to what we fear.

One Way to React to Fear is to Panic

I remember my first experience of floating in a swimming pool. I lay hesitantly on my back, all the while peeking to make sure my Dad's hand was still beneath me, ready to support me. When I felt his hand move away, I was afraid of drowning and I panicked, ruining my ability to float. So I tried again, this time attempting to relax. I had to let go of my fear, trusting that I'd be rescued if I started to sink. To concentrate on floating, I had to have *faith* that I wouldn't drown when my dad let go. And so I began to float, and when I did, I began to relax, and my fear completely disappeared. If I had stayed in my fear, I would never have learned to stay above water.

Panic is a negative response, a type of self-sabotage. It involves a transitional state, when fear becomes something out of control, and wildly dangerous. It keeps us in our fear, and prohibits learning and growth. Widespread panic can lead to confusion, chaos and other negative events. It can render the most efficient and effective person totally useless. It has the power to immobilize us.

Fear can be diminished by faith, which is a positive response. Another way to keep it from becoming panic is to hold on to our sense of order in the face of chaos. We can put our fears in perspective by asking, "What's the worst that can happen?" or even, "In five years from now, will this event be of any importance? Will I even remember it?"

The Gift of Fear

Fear is a brilliant internal guardian. It is nature's alarm system for danger. Real fear taps into our most potent energy reserves. It is a powerful ally, available to us whenever needed. In the presence of danger, it can propel us through risky situations, and can often save our life. But real fear is a warning that is intended to be brief, a survival signal. It is different from anxiety. Anxiety can be ongoing for weeks, months, or even years.

Most of us can name at least one or two things of which we are afraid, and sometimes it's good to be fearful. It is good that we are afraid of drowning. If we weren't afraid, on a very hot day we would jump into the cool water (the deeper the better), and if we couldn't swim, we would drown.

There are two rules concerning fear that, if implemented, can reduce its frequency, and transform our life experiences:

Rule #1: The very fact that we fear something is solid evidence that it is not happening.

Rule #2: What we fear is rarely what we *think* we fear—but what we *link* to fear.

Panic, an unmanageable kaleidoscope of fears, and the great enemy of survival, can be reduced by embracing the second rule. De Becker, in *The Gift of Fear,* uses the example of public speaking to explain the second rule. Believe it or not, public speaking ranks next to the fear of death on humanity's scale of fears. At first blush, this doesn't seem logical, but this is the path our minds take: when we fear public speaking, we are actually fearing our possible loss of identity, linked to performing badly. Our potential incompetence is further linked to loss of employment, family, and our ability to contribute to society, which is linked, in short, to our survival. In essence, we link public speaking to our ability to remain alive.

I am no stranger to fear. Most of my life, I was afraid of things other people would consider laughable. Having social phobia (see the following chapter), I was afraid of people—usually people I deemed superior to me, and any situation involving them. Imagine living like that! Many of my fears have dissipated since I've been in recovery, because I now have the tools necessary to conquer all my nonproductive feelings.

One of the first emotions I felt when I watched the hijacked airplanes slam into the World Trade Center on 9/11 was fear: fear for our nation; fear for what would happen next. It was the topic of conversation everywhere I went, and for good reason. By doing this, we found we were not alone in our emotional struggles. Discussing our fears helped take the power out of them.

Look at the benefits of the fear from that one event. Our nation is now much safer because of our fear. Air marshals have been added to many domestic flights, making air travel much safer today. We have a better response plan in case of attack. Our food supply, borders, and other means of travel have been scrutinized, making them safer, too. We used our fears to make our nation a much safer place to live.

One of the problems with fear, however, is that it can bring out our character defects, our shortcomings. Our imperfections are fear-based. Fear can cause dishonesty, physical problems, addictive behavior and many more negative qualities that potentially compromise our quality of life.

We can work to identify the fears that aggravate our character defects. By pinpointing these, we can work through them much more efficiently. This, by the way, is a lifetime undertaking, never completely finished.

According to Dr. John R. McGuaid, professor of psychiatry at UCSD, our beliefs are strongly determined by dramatic, attention-grabbing occurrences. Very often, our attention is drawn to spectacular, threatening information, and we ignore common contradictions. This leads us to inaccurate estimates of the likelihood of possible events. For example, we overestimate the chance of being infected by the bird flu, conversely underestimating our safety. Here, we find another acronym for fear—**F**alse **E**vidence **A**ppearing **R**eal. We spend a considerable amount of time wondering what we would do during a hijacking, when the probability of ever witnessing such an incident is less than winning the lottery (an event we overestimate). We can reduce our fears by trying to look at people, places and things as they really are, and not what we make them out to be.

When I used to snow ski, people who watched me told me that I fought the hill. The slope intimidated me, and I responded by dreading every irregularity or bump on the mountain. I slowed down, bracing for the worst, which inhibited my enjoyment, and by the end of the day, I was exhausted. I was defeating the purpose of being on the hill—I wasn't having fun. My fears had overwhelmed me. Soon, I learned to relax, and not panic. When I did, I found skiing much more pleasant.

The Certainty of Uncertainty

Fear arises when what we perceive as the status quo is threatened by change. But there is no such thing as the status quo. We change when we are born, we change when we die, and we are constantly changing every second in-between. Change is inevitable. We have either progression or regression, either growth or decay. Those of us who are fearful of change are fearful of the very essence of the universe!

Change is really only exchange. When something is taken away from us, we also gain something in return. When the functionality of Bill's body became compromised by his stroke, the spiritual aspect of his nature came alive. He had always been a good father, but he became much more family-oriented after his stroke. He became more interested in helping others, which in turn helped him to get out of himself.

We must accept change as an ongoing event, and use it to our advantage. When we deal with change in a positive manner, self-confidence and self-esteem are positive by-products. Finally, change can be exciting. Today, I find that not knowing what is going to happen next in my life is very exciting. I'm *inebriated* with the thought of what is just around the corner for me.

A few years ago, I wanted to study gerontology. San Diego State University had a program that was exactly what I was looking for, but the campus was almost an hour away, and I would have to hike another three-quarters of a mile across campus to get to my class after I got there. Immediately, my mind started in with all the fears. I would have to attend mid-winter. It would be dark, cold and rainy. How safe was it? Hadn't there been safety issues for women on campus in the past? What if something happened to my car on my way down there? There is terrible traffic at that one interchange—what if I was in an accident? How would I find my way around campus? My fears were hard at work trying to convince me not to go back to school and achieve my goals.

I had to jump-start my mind into looking at ways around any potential dangers. I had to put to use one of the best God-given skills for solving problems. I had to be creative. So I started thinking of ways to protect myself from any potential dangers.

I decided to go down to SDSU mid-afternoon, and see for myself what I was up against. I walked around and familiarized myself with the grounds, and I found the bookstore, the library, and where my first class would be. I asked fellow students about their experience on campus. I picked up a registration booklet and walked around some more. I thought of ways to ease my fears. One alternative was to take a class in the fall, before the darkness and rains came.

Groups of students sat talking and laughing on the grassy areas of SDSU. It is a beautiful campus, and nobody seemed afraid. Okay, this was beginning to seem more and more like a nice adventure. 'After all, we're supposed to be a little uncomfortable once in a while—that's how we grow,' I told myself.

The large parking garage, with its many floors, was frightening. I didn't like that at all, so I had to do additional thinking on that one.

While looking around, I noticed a large lot next to the big parking structure. It was open, and could be viewed from the bridge. I decided that I would park there. Now I felt a whole lot better, and so I enrolled, and started going to class. My first class was called "Biology of Aging," which was fascinating, and a perfect topic for this Baby Boomer. Once, I arrived in the classroom, I was so glad that I had made the effort to work through my fears. I was still uncomfortable, but at least I wasn't letting my fears keep me from what I wanted to do.

I would drive down in the daylight, arriving long before class was due to start, and use this time to do my written assignments. Driving back home at night, I had my cell-phone if I ran into trouble. I soon made some friends in my class, and if I didn't walk with them to my car, I sometimes walked with one of my teachers. In essence, I was now making my fears work for me.

Fear is a Great Servant but a Terrible Master

It is possible to learn to use fear to assist our purposes, rather than subjecting ourselves to its wantonness. As a woman who has spent 40 years running from my fears, I am well acquainted with the impact they can have on one's life. So I learned to channel my fears in a positive manner, and one by one, I conquered them. Now, each time I go through a painful situation without relapsing into self-destructive behavior, I grow stronger. I am building up a reserve of strength for future accessibility when needed. Today, most of my fears work for me, not against me.

Most of the time, the fear of the anticipated pain is worse than the actual unpleasant event, anyway. Bill had tons of fear after his stroke. Financial and health worries were two really big ones. What would he do with the rest of his life? How would we adjust to his disability? Would I fall apart? How would the kids react to their new dad? He did what I did, and we started to face our fears together, one by one. We didn't panic, but had faith that everything would turn out all right.

Worry Won't Relieve Tomorrow's Sorrow but Can Sap Us of Today's Strength

One form of misguided fear is worrying. Worrying is nonproductive. When we worry, we're focused on the problem, not the solution. Worry hurts us much more than it helps. It wastes time, and can even shorten our life.

Worry is a form of atheism, the human denial of God. When we worry, our fears work against us. Worry distracts us from our quest for solutions. Besides, what we dread rarely comes to pass in reality. Ninety percent of our confrontations in life are with imaginary enemies.

Worrying usually won't solve a thing, but will only serve to frustrate our potential creative flow. It misdirects our ingenuity. Worrying chokes off the imagination we need in order to find solutions. Our creativity turns to weeds, strangling our thoughts. Worry is a choice, and the creative genius that we so often apply to it can be used in far more productive ways.

Why do we worry? One reason is that it offers secondary rewards. Worrying sometimes gives us the illusion of solving the problem. We feel like we're working out a solution by worrying. Some people feel like they are exemplifying or providing love when they worry.

The relationship between real fear and worry is analogous to the relationship between pain and suffering. Pain and fear are necessary and valuable components of life. Suffering and worry are destructive and unnecessary components. Worry, suffering and anything that depletes our reservoir of energy for no good purpose must be forfeited, if we are to realize our potential and aspire to all the possibilities that our lives afford. We can't make the mistake of letting our creative thought process be crippled by anything counterproductive.

By controlling our thought processes, we can place limits on the amount of time spent worrying. When our mind is not distracted by empty fears, it can be released to be productive. It can be redirected into the problem-solving business.

Fear and Anxiety are Not the Same

The primary emotion that is present when we are experiencing anxiety is fear, but the two are not the same. Fear is only a part of anxiety. It is a subset. Anxiety may contain other emotions that are absent when we are experiencing pure fear. Excitement may appear if the end result of the anxiety appears to be positive. On the flip side, depression may kick in if the outcome appears negative.

Anxiety is so prevalent today that one psychiatrist has labeled it the great modern plague. There are four separate components involved when experiencing anxiety: our thoughts, emotions, physical sensations, and behavior. The combination and coordination of these components enable us to respond to perceived threats.

Periods of anxiety are usually mild, and limited in duration, but we have all had a few experiences of lengthy, intense anxiety.

Some people, however, experience 'pathological' anxiety, or an anxiety disorder. This occurs when the sensations of anxiety are excessively intense, last for longer than the situation warrants, or cause significant impairment in functioning. Pathological anxiety can be extremely distressing, and will be discussed further in the next chapter.

Most fears are rational and reasonable but, like the rest of our emotions, they are dual in nature. They can be either beneficial or detrimental to what we want to accomplish in our life. We must never give them the opportunity to hold us back, let them interrupt our growth, or keep us from living our lives.

Fear is simply lack of faith. And not relying on God makes our lives much more difficult than necessary. When I bring God to the forefront, I experience immediate relief. Practicing this reliance over time, our fears become more manageable. And like everything else, faith can be acquired by practice. When I first started attending 12-step meetings, I kept telling everybody that I was having trouble with my faith. Everybody kept telling me to act 'as if.' They told me to pray about it, even if I didn't believe. So I prayed and, to my amazement, it *did* work.

It took a while, but gradually I began to have faith. It did not return right away, but through practice, I became faithful again. Since then, my faith has matured, providing me with a multitude of dividends. Every time I manage to turn my fears over to God, I can freely and faithfully move on. Dwelling on God not only dispels fears, but also improves every experience I have.

The Anxiety-laden World of Social Phobia

We all need a certain amount of fear to survive, to keep us alert and from feeling too safe. Our nervous system is wired to allow for this oftentimes healthy emotional response, but sometimes our critical brain circuitry misfires. Our fears become phobias when they are irrational, interfere with everyday living, and keep us from doing the activities that we normally like to do. Phobias can prevent or disrupt taken-for-granted experiences of life, like walking down a crowded street, or flying in an airplane.

According to the American Psychiatric Association, phobias are the most common mental health problem in the United States today. At any given time, approximately 12% of Americans experience one of the more than 200 phobias that have been identified. Alphabetically, phobias range from ablutophobia (fear of washing or bathing) to zoophobia (fear of animals).

There are a number of theories as to what causes phobias, but they are most likely caused by a combination of factors. Most experts believe that phobias have to do with body chemistry and genetic predisposition. Relatives of people with anxiety disorders run a much higher risk of developing the same problem.

Regardless of the cause, there is a complexity inherent in attempting to understand and help people with psychiatric disorders. A person's genetic and biological makeup, his early experiences in life, his thoughts, feelings, sensations, and behaviors manifesting his anxiety, and the way that he copes, are unique to each individual.

Sufferers report a number of varying symptoms. Some people experience mental manifestations, while others exhibit physical responses. Mental symptoms include apprehension, intense fear, nervousness, and automatic negative thinking.

Normal anxiety may be unpleasant, but pathological anxiety is profoundly distressing. The bodies of sufferers of this disorder initiate the fight-or-flight response. Such physical reactions may include a racing heart, excessive dryness in the throat and mouth, muscle twitches, sweating, trembling, blushing, and a number of other bodily responses. Some phobics live with continual anxiety, while others only suffer brief, intermittent panic attacks. Those of us who are suffering from irrational fear cannot talk ourselves out of being afraid, even though the source is unreasonable or unknown.

Because panic attacks (phobic responses) are unexplained and unexpected, and we feel powerless in preventing them, they are often followed by anger or embarrassment. Then, because of our shame, we isolate ourselves from the very people who might be able to help us.

Because the physical and emotional pain for phobics is so extreme, it can cause loss of self-esteem. Unable to overcome our debilitating fear, we feel 'less than,' and incompetent. Much of the time that we spend away from the feared object or situation is consumed with dreading the next encounter, and developing elaborate strategies in an attempt to avoid the next excruciating event. The harder phobics work to avoid the things we fear, the worse the angst becomes.

There are three basic categories of phobias: specific phobias (fear of heights, snakes, etc.), social phobias, and finally agoraphobia (the fear of public places, the most disabling of all fears). Each type is different, but each causes strong, terrifying feelings.

Social anxiety or S.A.D. (Social Anxiety Disorder, not to be confused with Seasonal Affective Disorder) is the most prevalent phobia, but also the least understood. This type of anxiety affects 15 million Americans in any given year. It is the third largest psychological problem in the United States today, with one out of twenty people said to experience it. Unlike some other psychological problems, social anxiety is not well understood by the general public, or by medical and mental health-care professionals such as doctors, psychiatrists, psychologists and counselors.

For that reason, people with social anxiety are misdiagnosed almost 90% of the time. Let me repeat that—90% of the time! Another significant detriment to proper diagnosis of social phobia is that each of us is affected differently.

Because few socially anxious people are aware of their problem, and have rarely seen it discussed in the media, such as the television talk shows, they think they are the only ones in the whole world who have this debilitating fear. They feel they must keep quiet about it. They think it would be awful if anyone realized how much anxiety they experienced in daily life, and worry about what people will think of them.

Even though S.A.D. is the third leading psychiatric problem following depression and alcoholism, it has never been a major focus of psychiatry. Consequently, and unfortunately, without some kind of education, knowledge, and appropriate treatment, social phobia/social anxiety continues to wreak havoc in the lives of affected individuals. Adding to the dilemma, when a person with social anxiety finally gets up the nerve to seek help, the chances that they will find it are very, very slim. Lack of professional and knowledgeable therapists is the biggest and most relevant impediment to overcoming social anxiety.

Just about any activity that is near to people or that involves people is potentially threatening for sufferers of social phobia or S.A.D. It is characterized by an intense fear of social situations, where we may have to speak, perform or interact with others. With social phobia, instead of fearing specific things, the sufferer fears situations that require interaction with others. We dread meeting people, or being in the spotlight. We suffer tremendous anxiety before, during and after any social event. And the event can be as innocuous as meeting a friend for lunch.

Without treatment, social anxiety is a torturous emotional problem. Social phobia is a huge obstacle to our basic human need for social contact, and can cause considerable interference with everyday activities. It is well documented that people with social phobia are at greater risk of developing severe depression, panic attacks and substance abuse problems. Clinical reports suggest that individuals with S.A.D. often use alcohol to alleviate anxiety symptoms, a practice that leads to alcohol abuse and/or dependence in approximately 20% of affected individuals. Sufferers are also more likely to commit suicide.

Shyness is different from social phobia. I am not shy; people tell me I have a strong personality, and a great sense of humor. One of the biggest differences between social phobia and shyness is the intensity and duration. Shy people merely feel self-conscious. Social phobia elicits a much stronger reaction. It is persistent fear of criticism, rejection, and being scrutinized or humiliated by others. With a social phobic, the terror is severe and all-consuming. It commences long before the social experience, and is unremitting during the encounter.

One S.A.D. fact is that it wasn't until 1980 that social phobia became a recognized disorder. Before then, it would have been impossible to find a professional who understood my fears, much less treat them. By 1980, I had already been suffering from this disorder for 32 years, and was still unable to identify it. Social phobia was finally added to the list of recognized anxiety disorders in the 1986 revision of the Diagnostic and Statistical Manual of Mental Disorders (DSM-III), the official classification of mental disorders.

Every day of their lives, millions of people all over the world suffer from either a specific social phobia or a more generalized social phobia. A specific social phobia would be the fear of speaking in front of groups, whereas generalized social anxiety indicates that the person is anxious, nervous and uncomfortable in almost all (or the majority of) social situations.

People with S.A.D. usually experience significant emotional distress in the following situations: being introduced to other people; being teased or criticized; being the center of attention; being watched while doing something; meeting people in authority ('important' people); most social encounters, particularly with strangers; making 'small talk' at parties; and having to say something in a formal, public situation.

There is no known single cause of S.A.D., but research indicates that the disorder may be inherited. Most studies suggest a biological vulnerability, or a genetic predisposition. Quite frequently, this disorder surfaces in early adolescence, and can be crippling. Most of us are able to relate very well with familiar people, such as family and close friends, but our existence is restricted when S.A.D. motivates us in a negative way to avoid social situations.

A Very Cruel Disorder

If we have a phobia for snakes, we avoid snakes. It's as simple as that. How often does the average person encounter snakes, anyway? On the other hand, in order to live a full life, we must interact with others. We have to go to work, we have to go to school. We're forced to have 'people' encounters all the time, many times every day. If we have a social phobia therefore, we're in trouble. And because sufferers end up not doing well in social situations, their fears are reinforced with every experience. It becomes a vicious cycle of negative expectations and negative appraisals.

What makes the situation worse is that social anxiety does not come and go like other physical and psychological problems. If you have social anxiety one day, you have it every day for the rest of your life.

Some kids drop out of college because they're so terrified of being called on in class. They go on to miss out on jobs they're eminently qualified for because they're too terrified of the interview process.

My mom had a persistent fear of anyone outside the family, and her fear of humiliation or embarrassment incapacitated her. She was undeniably afraid of interaction with people. Nobody at that time (including medical professionals) knew that such an insidious condition existed, so even if she had identified that she had a problem, and had sought help, nothing could have been done for her.

She was a fabulous gardener, cook and seamstress. She was intelligent, and had a great sense of humor, but she couldn't talk to the neighbors without becoming extremely agitated. She was ambitious and clever, but S.A.D. permeated her life, drastically reducing her options. My life would eventually follow the same path. I couldn't make any sense out of her situation, but at the same time I completely identified with her. It was quite a conundrum, and I wouldn't get to the bottom of it until I myself had suffered for many years.

This disorder negatively impacted each of our lives. Fearing disapproval made most everyday activities unbearable for both of us. When I look back, I can see that I refused to do many things because of this irrational fear. I narrowed my talents and interests. Social phobia limited my life in profound ways, leaving me frustrated and confused.

Some social phobics remember that they were easily scared when they were children of four or five years of age. They hid from relatives who came to their home, or they could not speak in class.

Let me tell you about my early years, before I went off to school. My sister, Eileen, was two years older, and so we played together all the time. At the end of the day, she would tell all the stories, while I stood behind her, so excited but at the same time mortified, that all I could do was stand there with my mouth wide open flailing my arms. My parents and siblings didn't know what to think about my bizarre behavior.

Most kids look forward all year to their birthday, and the attention they'll receive. They cherish these precious events, where they are the star attraction.

Not me. I hated birthday parties, and couldn't figure out why others liked them so much.

Not long ago, I found a cute picture of me in a pinafore while browsing in one of our old family albums, which reminded me of my first day of school. I was on the second step of the school bus, and had just turned to wave to Mom. That morning, with my hair pulled back in two long perfect braids, my flawless skin glowed in the sunlight. What the camera didn't capture was the terror in my heart, caused by kindergarten jitters. I was venturing into the unknown, without my older brother and sister to lead the way.

I don't remember the fuss I must have made in the classroom, but I do recall waiting in the principal's office for my mom to pick me up. The year was 1953, and we only had one car. Since Dad used it for work, Mom had to trek over a mile to my school. I knew she'd be mad, but I held out hope that she'd find a smidgen of sympathy for her traumatized child. No such luck.

The walk home was the longest of my short life. With a few swats to my rear end, Mom let me know how upset she was. The next day, I chose school over my mother's anger and exasperation.

There must have been other events between kindergarten and high school. I always remember being much happier when I was outside, running around. If a physical activity was available, I was in the middle of it. It always relieved my anxiety.

S.A.D. didn't really accelerate until my teens. I remember around age fifteen my English Lit. instructor went around the room giving everyone a chance to read a paragraph from the novel we were studying. That shouldn't have seemed so difficult. I was a good student. I could read. But when it came to my turn I froze, and felt terribly awkward. I trembled, my voice quaked, and I almost burst out crying. How weird that I couldn't perform such a simple task? My focus of concern was not on reading the passage, but on whether my nervousness was evident, and what everyone was thinking about me.

I had an overwhelming feeling of inadequacy, and my mind went blank. Even though I always came well prepared for class, I would spend the whole time obsessing about being called upon— further compromising my performance. Being the center of attention was my worst nightmare. My trepidation was so evident in my unsteady and faltering voice that I wanted to escape, or break down in tears.

In my agitated state of mind, I couldn't pronounce a single word. I was so afraid, but stumbled through somehow, sweating and shaking the entire time. Normal anxiety wanes for most people when they begin to talk, but fails to diminish for social phobics— myself included. I was handicapped by it, and devastated by my insecurity. I felt weak. I was crippled. My life constricted. It began to close more and more doors for me without me ever realizing it.

A foreign language course was a requirement at my high school for those of us whose aspirations included college. There was no way I was going to recite, rehearse, conjugate or do anything else you had to do in Spanish or French classes. I solved that problem by taking Latin, because it wasn't a spoken language. Even though my friends took Spanish, I took Latin. I would rather take a class in the most difficult language than struggle through Spanish (the easiest) in front of the rest of my friends.

I researched the curriculum to determine which classes didn't require oral presentations. I became very good at math, and would have made a good teacher, but that career was quickly crossed off my list for obvious reasons. I realized that I would have to stand in front of a group of people on a regular basis. How could I teach if I couldn't talk without trembling?

I wouldn't share my terrifying fear of interacting with people with others because I was afraid everybody would think that I was very, very strange. I became an expert at covering up my disorder and pretending it didn't exist. I managed to erect invisible walls by restricting my activities. I was afraid to go to nice department stores, or to the beauty parlor, because the focus there would always be on me. 'Normal' people look forward to these types of experiences. They see them as enjoyable.

Rather than motivating us to do well, social phobia makes it impossible for us to perform. When I had a panic attack, I couldn't speak coherently with my desert-dry mouth. I couldn't hear anything over my pounding heart. I'd put syllables together in unintelligible jumbles. I was so completely focused on my problem that it disrupted my normal thought processes. I didn't want anyone to know how embarrassed I was, because it gave them even greater power. When asked to speak in class, the worst part for me was not whether my answer was right or wrong, but whether my fright would be revealed for everyone to see. My worst fear was that someone would discover my secret, and how absurd it was.

When I interacted with other people, the more status they had (or the more money or education), the more I fell apart. One of the worst circumstances was meeting people who I considered to be authority figures—bosses, supervisors, anyone who I considered 'better' than me in some respect. If they were higher on the social ladder, or had more money, or more things, I was a social cripple around them. I was so focused on not failing or giving myself away that I couldn't remember what had been said, and respond accordingly.

I had unbearable apprehension when speaking to teachers or bosses, which made it very difficult to express myself (I had to forget about ever asking for a raise). Introductions were impossible. Because introductions sent me into a state of panic in which I couldn't concentrate or remember names, I always flubbed them or depended on Bill to do them for me.

Job interviews were excruciating. During interviews, I knew I could do the job if I could just get past the interview process. Going to lunch was excruciating, even with friends. My hypervigilance turned me into a robot, at best. I couldn't enjoy the company of others, speak with ease, or empathize, because I was secretly practicing what I would say.

Parties, which my husband loved to throw and attend, posed another dilemma. Mingling was agony. My focus was always internal—how am I doing, etc.—so that I couldn't make heartfelt connections.

I wasn't deficient in social skills, and I needed the affection of other people, so I learned many ways to compensate and cope.

Some were detrimental to my health. I became very good at covering up my nervousness by appearing to be extroverted. I became known for my one-liners—my most comfortable way of communicating. I continued to suffer by never imagining that my acute anxiety was also experienced by other people. I was afraid that I'd be considered self-indulgent if I sought help. I was afraid of being told, "So what? Everybody gets nervous in front of a group. Get over it."

I dreaded going to work on days when meetings were scheduled, because I knew I'd have to speak in front of my coworkers. The anticipatory anxiety was heart-wrenching. I experienced a big wave of relief when the meeting was over, but I was convinced that everyone in the room saw how afraid I was.

I hated the first day of classes, because the professor would go around the room and we would have to introduce ourselves. Just sitting there waiting to be introduced in front of a roomful of strangers who would be staring at me was excruciating. My anxiety took hold of my entire being. I knew my voice would quiver, and I would sound scared and tentative. My thoughts were 'Why can't I perform this simple task?' Events such as these always left me feeling overwhelmingly vulnerable, powerless and inadequate. I always thought my symptoms were ridiculous, and held out hope that someday I would get over my social anxiety or outgrow it, but that never happened until...

Alcohol—A Blessing and a Curse

I desperately sought an escape—anything to get the upper hand over my intolerable everyday reality, but nothing offered any relief until later in my college years, I discovered that alcohol calmed my fears. I learned that when I couldn't avoid a situation, I managed it with alcohol, which was touted as a social lubricant. I had a cure, it was quick, and it worked for me for a long time. It was my own secret solution.

A stunningly stupid one, as it turned out.

Between my chronic low-grade depression and my social phobia, reality was *way* too difficult to face, but when I drank, I was finally at ease, and no longer depressed. I felt complete. Painful feelings disappeared. I felt confident, secure, calm and composed. All nervousness and anxiety faded away.

Alcohol was like magic. Gone was my self-consciousness. Down came the barriers between myself and others. I could talk easily without worrying about anything. I had found the cure for my anxiety. It was legal, and readily available.

But it was a short-term solution that had extremely detrimental long-term affects. Alcohol is addictive, and using alcohol in this manner can *increase* phobic episodes. I had fixed one problem, or so I thought, only to develop another.

There is a direct correlation between S.A.D and alcoholism. Since we self-medicate in an attempt to relieve our anxieties, seventy-five percent of people who suffer from S.A.D. become alcoholics. The converse is also true. Seventy percent of alcoholics suffer from anxiety problems.

According to experts in the field, it is very difficult for the sufferers of chronic anxiety to stop drinking unless they also get help for their anxiety. Beyond a doubt, that is why I couldn't stay sober. In addition to my chronic anxiety, I was now also a chronic alcoholic.

Over and over again, the treatment that was prescribed for my alcoholism was A.A. meetings. And guess what everybody is expected to do at A.A. meetings? That's right. Talk in front of a group of people!

Every time I walked into an A.A. meeting, I sabotaged my recovery. Most of the help that was offered for my alcoholism involved group therapy and group meetings, both of which were self-defeating measures. It was like putting paint thinner on an open sore. Not only was it not working, it was excruciating!

Science has found that the best way to address irrational fear is total immersion...except for social phobia. For many social phobics, this technique is not effective. I can attest to that. Facing my fear of public speaking never worked. My fear never went away, no matter how much I practiced. I never became comfortable interacting with groups of people. This is one instance where 'facing your fears' doesn't work. We have constantly faced our fears ever since birth (because we've had to), but our anxiety never subsides.

Today, there is a name for my condition—Social Anxiety Disorder. With S.A.D., the systems which regulate serotonin and dopamine, two neurotransmitters that are involved in the control of emotions, don't work properly. Many mental health experts use both medication and counseling to treat social phobia. Drug therapy has always been a treatment option. Before the introduction of selective serotonin reuptake inhibitors (SSRIs), the drugs most frequently prescribed were benzodiazepines such as Valium and Xanax, but these drugs posed problems of their own.

Most substance abuse treatment programs don't give initial psychiatric evaluations. Rehab centers tend to reject the idea that the patient might be suffering from two or more distinct disorders. Most counselors have experience with alcoholism, but no training in the treatment of other disorders.

Why wasn't my social phobia ever addressed? I've often thought about this. For one thing, I negated it by avoiding certain situations. And for a good part of my life, S.A.D. wasn't even recognized as a treatable condition.

My triple whammy (depression, social phobia and alcoholism) complicated my recovery from any one of them, causing me to relapse over and over again. By treating my alcoholism, my doctors were putting the cart before the horse, so to speak. My drinking was an outward response to my profound internal struggles. I used alcohol to quell my social discomfort, and not until I could conquer that could I ever conceive of living a normal life.

Today, we know that there is a relationship between the brain's biochemistry and mental disorders, and that proper medication has the uncanny ability to normalize brain imbalances. This process works to stabilize the patients' thoughts, feelings and, sometimes, their behavior.

SSRIs (these include the whole class of selective serotonin reuptake inhibitors such as Prozac, Paxil or Zoloft) serve to keep the proper amount of serotonin in the brain by preventing our body from reabsorbing it. These drugs help correct faulty brain chemistry known to trigger some phobias and depression. Drug therapy was the solution for me. There are side effects to these drugs, but for me, the advantages far outweigh the disadvantages. A low dose of an antidepressant kick-started my recovery from alcoholism, because it treated my depression and social anxiety, so there was no longer any reason for me to self-medicate. With my depression and S.A.D. in remission, my substance abuse quickly followed suit.

It's critical that people with social anxiety be made aware of all available treatments, for there can be a better life, after all. Social anxiety disorder is among the most treatable of all mental conditions, but the difficulty is that most social phobics are just too fearful to ask for help. Sufferers find themselves in a catch-22 situation. There is no way out, other than asking for help, but the very nature of the disorder prevents many people from getting treatment. Only 15% of people with serious social phobia seek medical help, making it one of the most under-treated of all psychiatric disorders.

Today, therapy, counseling and a low dose of Paxil have relieved my social phobia and my depression significantly. Hallelujah! My despondency and fear of social situations have been wiped out forever!

It was such a tremendous relief just knowing I had a distinctly recognizable disorder that was shared by many others. I was not alone, and had a treatable, controllable condition. I was really not that strange.

"With treatment for all of their disorders simultaneously and appropriately, patients can exchange a life of chaotic misery for one of happiness and freedom…bringing an end to the 'revolving door' of relapses and recidivism. When patients are treated for only one of their illnesses at a time, the relapse of the other ailments will precipitate a relapse back into all three." (p. 245, *Masquerade, Unmasking Dual Diagnosis,* by Richard A. Morin, M.D.)

After I received treatment for all my mental and emotional disorders, I finally began to live. Never in my wildest dreams had I ever imagined that today I could feel this good about myself and my relationships with other people. I can now step forward with confidence into any social situation, from going to lunch with a friend to giving a speech in front of a large group of people. That is one magnificent recovery!

That is my story.

The following pages are devoted to the joyous outcomes of my experiences and how you can take advantage of what I've learned. My gleaned knowledge has made all the difference in my life, may it do the same for yours.

Part Two

Discovering Joy

How am I Doing as a Human Being?

We are all messy mortals...every single one of us. There is no getting around the fact that we are flawed, so it is our responsibility to improve on our situation. Are we getting better, or are we getting worse? Our efficiency and effectiveness can be examined on a regular, ongoing basis by frequent personal checkups or continuous self-monitoring so that we can make the most of our capabilities.

This self-searching (so to speak) brings the dark or negative side of our nature to light, enabling us to clean out the toxic stuff. It also helps us examine or analyze our own thoughts and deeds, empowering us to access our unique strengths and abilities. In the 12-step recovery program, it's called 'taking inventory.' We list our assets but, more importantly, we write down our liabilities. This helps us sort out the good, the bad and the not-so-good.

Let's look at self-improvement for a minute, purely from a selfish standpoint. We are the only person we know for sure that we will live with for the rest of our life. Do we want to live with a dud or a louse? No, we want our constant companion to be the most outstanding person available, someone who will afford us the best life possible. But there's only one way to do that, and that is to work hard to become the best we can be.

If we don't take a look at ourselves on a regular basis to determine where we are going, life will quite possibly take us places we never wanted to be. This ongoing process of uncovering and discovering our ever-changing selves brings our attention to detrimental areas in our lives that need to be discarded. As we obtain new knowledge, we revise our understanding of ourselves to include this, and change our life plan if it no longer applies.

The Harder We Work on Ourselves, the Easier Life Will Be

M. Scott Peck states in *Further Along the Road Less Traveled* that it is his belief that the greatest positive event of the 20th century occurred on June 10, 1935, when Dr. Bob and Bill W. convened the first A.A. meeting in Akron, Ohio. This group marked the beginning of the self-help movement, when it integrated science and spirituality at the grassroots level. It also marked the beginning of the community movement. This self-help movement has taught us to take ownership and responsibility for ourselves. From that, all of our lives have been enriched.

Before the self-help movement was established, spending too much time on oneself was considered self-indulgent. But if we don't take a good hard look at ourselves, how can we make improvements? How can we be the best we can be?

Our Lives are Like Motion Pictures... Always Changing

Change is the essence of the universe, and one of the laws of life. Change keeps things interesting. It is the zest of life. The changes that occur in our lives on a regular basis are great opportunities to learn and grow. Minor annoyances keep us in shape to better handle catastrophic events. They give us practice. If we are alert for them, anticipate them and embrace them, they won't overwhelm us, but will serve to educate us, instead.

Our four dimensions (physical, mental, emotional and spiritual) are like rivers...not stagnant, but constantly changing. Our bodies are always working, never standing still. For that reason, if we aren't moving forward (growing), we are surely falling behind (diminishing).

But growth can be difficult. In order to grow, we must master the unpredictable crises of life. When we conduct a life of continuous and unending stringent self-examination to evaluate how we are changing and who we are becoming, it is much easier to stay on course to reach our goals, for life serves us up its best lessons when we least expect them.

Being proactive helps keep us in control. It helps prepare us for when the pressure is on, and our world is blown apart. Being proactive includes stretching our limits on a regular basis, and forcing ourselves to move past our comfort zones, for if we don't, our lives will shrivel.

We must never succumb to a 'comfort coma.' To continue to learn and grow, we have to be a little uncomfortable as often as possible, because those difficult places are usually ideal situations for optimum growth. But we don't like to be uncomfortable. Therein lies our challenge. But how much growth do you suppose happens on an afternoon that involves a bag of chips, a can of beer, a clicker and the couch?

A fulfilling life is a life with ongoing struggles to reach new heights. We are born with the desire to maximize our talents and potentialities, and to consciously improve ourselves by being proactive. This uniquely human and precious tool enables us to strive for continual improvement. Our challenge is to use this gift to its utmost.

Emotions Are Meant to Be Felt

There are other tools to help us in our self-evaluation process. Emotions can signal areas of our life that need improvement. They are there to warn us of misdoing, or to make us aware of what needs to be done. Emotional intelligence is the innate potential to feel, use, communicate, recognize, remember, learn from, manage and understand our feelings. The chances of us handling matters appropriately improve if we are emotionally astute.

Emotions are essential human attributes, and if we deny our emotions, we diminish our humanness. As humans, we have the ability to *observe* when we are angry, fearful, glad, or sad. When we recognize these emotions, we are better able to bracket them when need be, reframe them, and master them. The art of reframing redefines a situation so that it is less threatening. The event hasn't changed, but our perspective of it has.

Since all of our emotions serve a purpose, we cannot value only the good ones. When we experience painful emotions, because we want the comfort of contentment, our immediate reaction is to get rid of them, or repress them somehow. By doing this, we'll never learn what's driving the way we feel.

Feelings are opportunities to find out about ourselves, and the observance of them helps us to gauge where we're at on our life journey. Emotions such as sadness and fear are essential parts of our personalities, and can provide a great source of motivation to accomplish important tasks. We own our feelings. They are not meant to enslave. They are meant to be mastered for our enrichment and benefit. If we don't use them to work for us, then they will surely work against us.

Let me relate this to owning a pet. Domesticated animals can provide us with affection, spontaneity, and a better quality of life, so we keep them around and take care of them. But we don't let them play on the kitchen table, where we eat our meals.

We would be slaves to our pets if we didn't control them. We let them know who is boss by setting limits and giving them structure. I nurture my cats because I love them, and they help to satisfy some of my needs, but if they were to run rampant, there would be chaos and confusion all around, destroying the purpose of having them at all.

The same idea can be applied to our emotions or feelings. We must treat them with respect. We should listen and respond to them, but we should also organize, limit and sometimes redirect them.

HALT is an acronym that is used quite often in 12-step recovery programs. It stands for **H**ungry, **A**ngry, **L**onely and **T**ired. The program teaches us that when we are experiencing any of these, it's a good time to pause, because in this state we're probably not going to make good choices. Because I understand and appreciate my body today, because I know my limits and honor my body clock, I stop and take care of myself if I'm feeling hungry, angry, lonely or tired. Any of these conditions leave me vulnerable to my shortcomings. It sounds simple, but I and many others don't always take time to recognize our basic needs.

Just as certain plants require a dormancy period to gain strength for regrowth, so is rest necessary for our mental, psychological, spiritual and biological health. This necessary respite helps us to gather wisdom, and improves our overall health. It gives us time to rejuvenate. At the hospital district where I work, we have complicated computer programs that require regular downtime in order to work correctly. During this time, problems are identified and repaired. Our bodies work in a similar fashion.

Sometimes, the best bridge between despair and hope is merely a good night's sleep. During this 'downtime,' our subconscious mind processes our daily activities, and we gain a better perspective. Rest and renewal empowers us to move forward on an upward spiral of growth and continuous improvement.

The Critical Interval

There's always a small interval of time between an event and our reaction to it. Sometimes, that's all we have, and it can make all the difference in the world. At that initial point in time, we can either choose to wallow in our misery, or take the sometimes difficult steps to work our way out of it. Depending on the way we respond to an event, we become weaker and sicker, or we become stronger and healthier.

Hundreds of different situations serve to program our attitudes every day, and negative thoughts are inevitably going to creep into our minds. The key is to be prepared with a game plan that responds offensively and defensively as appropriate, rather than one that merely reacts.

When we react, little thought is given to long-term consequences. Not enough time has transpired to enable us to fully process our emotions. Reacting rarely does anything to improve the situation, and can often make it worse. When we are angry, anxious, vindictive, or envious, it is impossible to think and act wisely.

When we respond, we slow down long enough for our brain to become fully engaged, and our self-awareness is high. We have the long-term picture in mind. When we take a step back, we can look at events objectively to better analyze them and interpret them for our benefit.

In a highly mobile, fast-changing, and complex society, the ability to recognize our feelings as they come over us (self-awareness) is critical to enable us to gauge our ability to handle the situation properly. If we're unhappy, we know to look for the problem in at least one of the four areas that comprise our being. Once we become aware of our emotional response, we have a better chance of dealing with it correctly. That's using emotional intelligence.

Even when we are angry, we can develop the ability to bracket our feelings long enough to realize that we are angry, and then choose better how to respond. This allows us to remove ourselves from the situation long enough for our intelligence to intervene appropriately so that our anger won't cause us to react irrationally.

When we respond, we make a positive and constructive mental adjustment. When we respond, we channel the energy of the negative emotion into a positive attitude and action. Choosing to respond, rather than reacting, helps us stay in control of our attitude and our life.

Let me give an example of how I change immediate reactions to more productive responses. It's Tuesday, and I'm leading the best possible life I can live. Things are humming along, I love my work, I work for a good company, love the people I'm working with, and at the same time I'm providing a service for people. Life is good, my kids are grown and pursuing their own careers, and I've got free time to pursue other interests, like writing and helping others. I've been taking care of myself by walking, going to the gym, and eating right, so on my way to the doctor's office, I'm pumped. The visit goes well. Height and weight hasn't changed—that's always good. Blood pressure is 100 over 68, with pulse 56. I'm very proud of myself by now. She hands me the paperwork to have blood drawn for a couple more tests, and I'm out the door and flying high.

All the blood work comes back normal and the bone scan is scheduled in a couple of weeks. I'm so proud of myself for taking such good care of myself. I'm so busy patting myself on my back that my arm hurts. My life continues to hum along again, and I take the bone scan and the results come back, and I'm stopped dead in my tracks—I'm diagnosed with osteopenia—and I am off-the-charts angry!

The itty-bitty committee that lives right above my eyebrows is telling me. 'This can't be right. I'm taking my calcium, I'm doing weight-bearing exercises, I'm getting plenty of vitamin D.' I am angry, disappointed and feeling way out of sorts. I'm not thinking right, and not as happy-go-lucky as I'm used to being. As a matter of fact, I'm mad! Now, I could react in a number of inappropriate ways (I'm good at that). I could say the hell with it, and go out and buy a quart (probably more) of Krispy Kreme bread pudding, but I've learned to recognize this state of mind, and I've also learned to think it through.

So I breathe, and wait for my initial *reaction* to subside, because I know it will. I also know I can't do anything reasonable while I'm upset. So, I go about my daily business, talk to my husband (my immediate resource) about it, and start to gather ideas as to how best to address this situation. I start to develop a plan, while I continue to digest my new health status, which I still can't believe.

While I'm doing this, I notice something. I'm beginning to calm down. I'm beginning to realize that this is not a death sentence. I'm beginning to feel *grateful* that I live in the 21st century, and that modern technology is able to detect that I might be developing a problem. Secondly, I begin to realize that there are solutions to my health threat.

The doctor, I remembered, jotted a note on the test telling me that we could address this issue during my next office visit. For me, that's another whole year! I don't like that idea at all, so I take *responsibility* for my own health care, call my doctor, and ask for her next available appointment. I'm beginning to feel even better now, because once again, I've responded appropriately. I've changed a nonproductive reaction into a correct response.

Our Secret Power

A positive attitude causes a chain reaction of positive thoughts, events, and outcomes. It is a catalyst and it sparks extraordinary results.

— Wade Boggs

Our attitudes drive our actions and, to a certain degree, even control the direction our lives will take. They are a tremendous force, working 24 hours a day, for good or for bad. For this reason, it is of paramount importance that we know how to harness and control our attitude. This priceless possession governs the way we perceive the world, as well as the way the world perceives us, and is the first thing people notice about us.

We are given the ability to observe our attitudes in order to identify those that hold us back, and those that propel us forward. When we discover the detrimental attitudes, we can manipulate them to better serve us. One way to better our attitude is to become solution-oriented. When we focus on what we want to do, and where we want to be, our attitudes improve. Another way to shatter a bad attitude is to focus on the possibilities of tomorrow. If we take a long-term perspective, and understand that what is happening right now is only a temporary thing, we will be less likely to become embittered, or to form a negative attitude. One easy way to become positive is to develop our gratitude muscle (see the chapter on happiness).

We go for physical checkups and dental checkups, and our cars get regular tune-ups, but rarely do we think to check up on our attitudes, even though those of us with better attitudes generally enjoy better health. Just as we build a better body through physical exercise, we build a better attitude by mental exercises.

The people who do best in life are those who realize they have a choice of attitudes, just like they have a choice of companions, meals, cars and clothes. We can learn to use whatever tools we've found to help our attitude. Exercise, humor and being around other positive people usually help my attitude. I frequently use all three. When we have good attitudes, we are positive, dynamic people-magnets with increased potential for achieving great things.

We are not negative when we arrive in this world. Negativity is a learned behavior. And if we've learned it, we can unlearn it. A bad attitude can cripple our ability to fulfill our potential. Studies indicate that people who express negative emotions (such as anger) do not live as long as people who convey positive emotions (such as enthusiasm). It is a scientific fact that positive emotions help to combat illness and block disease.

Our attitude supports or sabotages everything we do. It either keeps us going, or cripples our progress, fuels our fires, or assaults our hope. We can choose an attitude that will help us deal with challenges, overcome obstacles and accomplish our goals, or we can choose an attitude anchor that slows us down, holds us back, or even stops us altogether. The decision is ours.

Did I have a Bad Day or did I have a Bad Five Minutes that I Milked All Day?

If we must indulge in negativity—let's set a time limit on it. A nasty attitude can be turned into an attitude of gratitude by once again shifting our perspective. Let's reframe our bad attitude by using one of the following questions: 'Will the current situation last forever?' Probably not. 'Will it ruin our whole life?' Probably not. 'Does this happen to everybody?' Probably.

Becoming an optimist consists of learning a set of skills that are readily available. Our attitude can be coaxed from negative to positive by learning to coach our self-talk, and the more we practice positive thinking, the more instinctive it becomes.

We all endure hardships that have the ability to either bring out the worst in us, or inspire the best. It all comes down to the attitude we choose. There's no barrier too high, no valley too deep, no dream too extreme, no challenge too great that the right attitude can't overcome.

We are What we Repeatedly Do

If we want to improve ourselves, then we have to work on our habits. Excellence is derived from a series of good habits. But what are good habits? Good habits are habits where the psychological payoffs outweigh the drawbacks. Good habits build self-esteem, and boost our effectiveness. They produce positive benefits, actions, and attitudes in our lives. If we develop good habits, our life will improve. It's as simple as that. We can master our habits, and replace self-defeating ones with more effective ones that will propel us toward our goals and our dreams.

We would pay more heed to the formation of habits if we realized the extent to which we are mere walking bundles of them, both good and bad. We unconsciously shape all four of our dimensions (physical, mental, spiritual and emotional) every day by our eating, drinking, sleeping, exercising and other habits.

Habits can solve problems, or they can be the problem. They can maximize or minimize our opportunities. Good habits empower, while bad habits leave us powerless; and the best way to get rid of bad ones is to develop good ones.

Even Perfectionists Aren't Perfect

None of us will ever be perfect, and we can add that to our gratitude list. Imagine how bored we'd be with nothing to strive for. Being imperfect gives us the opportunity to laugh at ourselves. Besides, excellence doesn't require perfection.

There is a huge difference between being a perfectionist and working on ourselves on a daily basis in order to become better people. Life is not about perfection, but about crafting ourselves in such a manner that when the unavoidable times of anguish arrive, we will be better able to diminish our suffering.

Perfectionistic tendencies can be self-defeating and distressing. The idea that anything short of perfection is unacceptable can cause major distress, and bog us down. By dwelling on impossible goals, we very often miss the simple pleasures of life.

Perfectionism is doing things that keep us from accomplishing more important things in life. It causes obsessive-compulsive behavior, and there are even people in recovery from it. Perfectionists miss lunch with their friends because they couldn't get the kitchen counter clean enough, and they are late to work because they couldn't find the right outfit.

God doesn't expect us to be perfect, so why should we demand it of ourselves? When we look at our most embraced prayers, none of them ask for faultlessness.

There is a popular prayer that I try to bring to mind when I need guidance in how to handle myself. It goes like this:

"Teach me, my Lord, to be gentle in all events, especially in disappointments. Let me put myself aside, to hide my little pains and heartaches so that I may be the only one to suffer from them. Let me use the suffering that comes across my path that it may mellow, not embitter me; that it may make me patient, not irritable; that it may make me broad in forgiveness, not narrow, haughty, or overbearing."

Nowhere does the author of this prayer ask God for perfection. We don't ask, because we know it's not going to happen.

It seems counterintuitive, but imperfections can be great motivators. Let's take a look at Demosthenes, one the greatest Greek orators of all time. He lived from 384 to 322 B.C. but the story of his life is still meaningful today. When Demosthenes was a youth in ancient Athens, he had a terrible speech impediment. People jeered at his stammering when he spoke publicly. No one could have believed that he would become the greatest of the Greek orators, but get this—he did not become a successful orator despite his deficiency. Demosthenes took a positive attitude toward his limitation and became a great orator because of it! Upon realizing that his harsh, unpleasant voice and awkwardness was a barrier to his success, he became determined to fix it.

To learn to speak with clarity, he practiced talking with a mouth full of pebbles. He developed the *habit* of working hard to be understood. He had to exaggerate his enunciation. His voice was weak, so he strengthened it by shouting over the roar of ocean waves. Because he had to try harder than everybody else, he became that much better than everybody else. Eventually, he became one of the greatest orators of all time!

After recognizing and accepting our imperfections, we can take steps to correct them, or adjust our life map to accommodate them. Our limitations can turn out to be advantages, especially if we encourage them to work for us, rather than against us.

For me, there is nothing more beautiful than watching someone take a crippling disadvantage and not only overcome their disability, but turn it into a benefit. There is nothing more inspiring than to hear about someone who has taken a minus and turned it into a plus.

Everybody on Earth has some sort of weakness, and if we think we don't, then pride (the greatest shortcoming of all) is our weakness. To a certain degree, we are fortunate when our weaknesses bring us to our knees, demanding our full attention. We are forced to find a solution, and to take the time to recover, if necessary.

When we study the lives of the most accomplished people, we see they have troubles just like everybody else. Many even have *more* problems than the norm. In spite of these, they don't consider themselves victims. Instead, they are victors. The key was in their decisions, not their conditions.

We are the Architects of Our Future

The person best suited to improve my life, change my attitude, elevate my standards, and overcome my limitations, is me. Today, I am in charge of designing my life, and I intend to design it to count for something.

God has given us a beautiful garden of opportunity to cultivate. We pull the weeds (harness our shortcomings) so that the blooms (our potential) will have room to grow. We can't grow if we ignore our faults and wrongdoings, but it is because of the pain involved in genuine self-examination that many people never even consider it.

Let's look at the four areas of our lives represented as the sides of a simple box. All four sides are interdependent, and yet each side has a unique purpose. When one part caves in or falls apart, the entire box ceases to function properly, and this can lead to total collapse. Just like the sides of a box, when one of our human dimensions break down, it affects the other three. Neglect any one area of our life in any respect, and we negatively impact the rest of it.

These four dimensions give balance to our minds and bodies. Our systems stay in sync through these daily adjustments and recoveries. As we improve in one area, we increase our ability to improve in other areas, as well. The nurturing of each of these areas impacts our creative energies, and we are propelled onward by a tremendous positive synergy of effectiveness.

Our spiritual needs must be validated as equally important and fundamental for our existence as our physical, mental and emotional aspects. Spirituality and its sometimes invisible potential is a fundamental part of human existence.

Another tool to help us determine how we're doing is to check our perspective. Unlike animals, we can see not only everything around us, but we can also take a look at our perspective (*how* we see and interpret the world).

The way we perceive things is like a template with which we traverse life, and our perception affects our attitude. The more accurate our perception of the world, the better equipped we are to deal with reality, and the more manageable our lives will be. We must accept and even welcome challenges to our perception of reality if we are to grow in wisdom and effectiveness.

In the early stages of our life, a large portion of our time is spent learning and obtaining knowledge. In order to grow, we must continually expand our realm of knowledge, adjusting our field of vision (perspective) as we glean new information. Learning means giving up old ideas. We must be willing to abandon our narrow perspective in order to grow.

When our perception is askew, progress is difficult. Take, for example, a maze with one transparent wall. At first glance, we think that going through that wall is an easy way toward our destination. Upon closer inspection however, we realize our view is faulty. The invisible wall is not a way to our destination at all. We must change our way of thinking by remembering the barrier, or we'll keep running into it every time. By identifying hazards and taking action to avoid them, we can find and cling to the right course.

The more 'reality checks' we perform and revisions we make, the more accurate our life maps will be, and the easier our journey will be. Sometimes, when enough new information is accumulated, we must make some very big revisions. The biggest revision I had to make in my thinking was in recovery. I had to learn to see that the world was not a threatening place, but one filled with love. One of the benefits I've observed by improving myself is that the more I work on myself, the more I attract people who are doing the same. And ongoing collaboration is one of the key elements for real success, since dynamic people tend to build each other up (see the next chapter titled *Authentic Success).*

Within each of us, there exists two people—who we are today, and who we are going to be in the future, based on our experiences and our responses to them. What we perceive and act upon today sets the pattern for how we will deal with the coming supreme sorrows and temptations that will surely fall upon us at some point in the future.

So, how are we doing? Are we recovering from our latest setback? Are we arriving at a proper understanding of events? If we are, we are not only growing, but we are feeling really good about it at the same time.

Authentic Success

Earl Nightingale, one of the greatest philosophers of the 20th century, said in *The Strangest Secret* that "Success is the progressive realization of a worthy ideal," a worthy ideal being a goal of great value. With that in mind, let's look at what happened in my neighborhood a number of years ago.

A husband and wife who lived around the corner from us wanted to downsize, since their kids had all grown and moved out. Their house was one of the more expensive ones in the area and at the time, the home was a showplace. Nothing really needed to be done. They sold it quickly, since the real estate market was hot, and so I thought the story was over.

Pretty soon, however, we noticed that the new owners had six to eight trucks lined up in their driveway with the same number of 100-foot palm trees and heaps of sod to be planted where ice plant used to be. To all of this, the new people added fountains and all kinds of extravagant, ostentatious amenities.

The people who had sold the house happened to be the parents of Vicki, a good friend of mine, and so all along, Vicki kept me posted as to what was going on.

"Would you believe the buyers paid cash for that house," she said, expressing her disbelief.

"You're kidding. What does he do?" I asked, wanting to know why he was so *successful.* "Would you believe that he imports tires?"

"Tires? What are they made of…gold?"

"I told my parents he's probably using them to smuggle cocaine," she kidded, and we both laughed.

Fast forward to six months later. The house was now looking like the Taj Mahal. It was so incredibly ostentatious that the kids in the neighborhood had taken to calling it 'the drug dealer's house.'

One evening a few months later, I was preparing dinner with one ear and eye on the nightly news when they interrupted the regular stuff with breaking news. One of the biggest drug kingpins in the country had been arrested right here in San Diego—in Rancho Bernardo, no less. They showed footage of the house where the arrest had been made, and it was the Taj Mahal—'the drug dealer's house!'

The new owner of the house and his wife ended up in jail, along with over one hundred of their 'friends.' So, what looked to be sweet success turned out to be its mighty antithesis. Our new neighbors had all the trappings of wealth, but weren't successful at all. In the end, they were ultimate failures.

What I'm exemplifying here is that being wealthy is not the same as being successful. Success is not the accumulation of inert matter. Money is merely a resource—albeit a powerful one—to be used either for good or for evil. Just look at what happened on 9/11. It took a lot of money to cause such massive destruction and human anguish. So, it's not what we've got that makes us successful, but what we continue to do with what God has given us. Money is a means, not an end. It only counts when it's put to good purpose.

I like what William Jordan has to say on page 39 of *The Majesty of Calmness*:

> *"How will I let poverty or wealth affect me? If that trial or deprivation has left me better, truer, nobler, then poverty has been riches, failure has been a success. If wealth has come to me and has made me vain, arrogant, contemptuous, uncharitable, cynical, closing from me all the tenderness of life, all the channels of higher development, of possible good to my fellow man, making me the mere custodian of a money-bag, then wealth has lied to me, it*

has been failure, not success; it has not been riches, it has been dark, treacherous poverty that stole from me even myself."

Authentic success is not a destination. It is a PROCESS that includes: *Perseverance, Resilience, Openness, Compatibility, Enthusiasm, Self-esteem,* and finally, *Spirituality.*

My husband, Bill, was a very successful man at the peak of his career when he suffered a massive stroke in 1993. Did this stroke make him a failure? Quite the contrary. Today, he is *as* successful and maybe *more* successful than he was before his cerebral hemorrhage. He is still successful because he assessed the situation, reviewed his options and got into action. Instead of narrowing his world, his brain aneurysm caused him to grow in previously neglected areas of his life, and today the dimensions of his success have expanded!

People today don't stop and say, "Oh, look at poor Bill. He had everything going for him, and then look what happened." That never enters their minds. They're saying, "Boy, look at him go. He is one incredible man."

All the habits that made him successful in the first place carried over after his stroke. He practiced *Perseverance, Resilience, Openness, Compatibility, Enthusiasm, Self-esteem,* and last, but far from least, *Spirituality* to recover from his setback. As a matter of fact, he exhibits these qualities more now than ever before.

Perseverance

The ability to stick with a project or situation until it is completed regardless of setbacks and disappointments. To succeed, we must plan, research, seek advice, collect information, develop the right skills, and prepare thoroughly for when the all-important opportunity comes along. Success in many things comes word-by-word, step-by-step, or stroke-by-stroke. Nothing is mastered in one giant leap forward. It usually takes planning, preparation and practice. It requires modifications and adjustments in both thought and action, not just once, but over and over again.

But if we work hard, good things will happen. The ability to go on and do something, even if we don't feel like doing it, will take us one step closer to our goal. To be a function of our dream, and not a function of our immediate desires or impulses, will empower us to reach our potential. If we want to be successful, we will have to work patiently and persistently, taking a step at a time in order to continually grow.

Often, we have to do what we like least to get what we want most. What many of us like least is waiting, but patience is a part of persevering. Patience is a choice, and a vital form of perseverance.

A certain amount of impatience is good, because it creates the intensity you need to keep everything going, but too much impatience is often counterproductive. When impatient or in a hurry, our work becomes sloppy, and has to be redone.

Patience allows us to deal effectively with other people. It's a lot about what we don't do. It's about not exploding when we really want to, about putting up with something, or waiting for something to happen, rather than forcing it along. Patience allows us to be more effective with our family. It allows us to have a successful relationship with our in-laws.

More patience equals less stress. Patience not only makes us healthier and happier, but also increases the chance that we'll get what we want. One way to cultivate patience is to separate what is truly important to us from the things that make little or no difference. What will really happen if we miss that deadline, or if this traffic jam makes us an hour late?

Back in the 1940s, when Winston Churchill was the number one man in the British Empire, he addressed an Oxford graduating class. When the great man stepped up to the microphone—with the audience expecting the usually long and very dull commencement address—Churchill looked out over the crowd of young faces and said, "Never, never, never, never, never, never give up." He then turned and walked back to his seat. That was all he said! (*Miracle of Change*, p. 80)

I thank God everyday for the gift of 'stick-to-it-iveness' He has so graciously bestowed upon me. Perseverance has allowed me the successes I now enjoy, and continue to build on every day.

Resilience

The ability to roll with the punches, to deal effectively with life's adversities.

When we're forced to take a step down that famous ladder we all like to climb, in order not to be defeated we must rest, regain our balance, rethink our previous tries, and get a second wind. We can think of these setbacks as guideposts, not hitching posts. We can use them as stepping stones, not stumbling blocks. Failures give us the opportunity to regroup, but we must not become stuck. When denied or rejected, we must not cry so hard that our vision is blinded. Failure is merely a part of the learning process, and a much better teacher than success.

In the course of my life, I have failed many times at many things, but each time I embraced the lesson and moved on, keeping in mind that failure is one of God's educators. I've made my failures propel me, giving me power and impetus.

Vince Lombardi, the famed football coach, described failure another way. He said that 'It's not whether we get knocked down, it's whether we get back up again.' Success is about mistakes well-handled. It's about overcoming obstacles with courage, imagination and good humor as our journey continues to evolve. No one who is following a dream has ever taken a direct, unobstructed path. It can be a bumpy road, full of twists and turns, and littered with obstacles and setbacks.

We can learn about the success of failure from football. What do running backs do when they are tackled? They purposely fall forward. When they are taken down, they want to end up as close to the goal as they can. They want to gain as much as they can from the last play. They want to set their team up...not set it back. It's not about failing, but about failing forward.

We can learn the proper way to process failure. We can be mindful and self-monitor our thinking by watching out for that defeatist attitude. Failure is inevitable, but it need only be a temporary position; giving up is what makes it permanent. It offers the opportunity to begin again more intelligently, and it can serve to sweeten our victory. We can look at failure not as the finish line, but as a provider of important lessons that cannot be found elsewhere. It's about looking for the gift, and profiting from our loss.

In order to succeed, we must use our reversals and make them work for us. What we see as failure may actually be a step closer to success. We now know what doesn't work. At this point, we should analyze our defeat and put the lessons learned toward our next move. Many of us quit right when advancement is imminent, when winning may mean trying again just one more time.

Whether we like it or not, we are all veterans of failure. To be successful, we must accept failure as a right of passage, or look at it merely as success postponed. Thomas A. Edison once said that every wrong attempt discarded is another step forward. We can look upon defeat as secret information, firsthand experience we previously lacked. We can then go on and exploit this power. We are liberated from the encumbrances which defeat has revealed to us, and one step closer to success with our next attempt.

Experimental science is almost all failure until the moment of breakthrough. Researchers have failed to find a cure for many diseases since we declared war on them, but do you think these scientists are about to give up? No way. They know they are closer than ever before, because the failures they've experienced have enabled them to narrow their search.

Many new discoveries have been made when scientists were looking for something else. One of the most famous new drugs of the last decade, Viagra, was thought to be a treatment for angina, but failed miserably as such. However, while being tested in clinical trials, scientists discovered another valuable use for the drug. While Viagra proved to be useless as a treatment for angina, the researchers began to get reports of some unexpected side effects...

Resilience is critical in times of change, and the times are always changing (every day, every hour, every minute, every second). When times get tough, resilient people face the challenges and analyze their options in order to gain a clearer perspective of what they need to accomplish. Many become more spiritual, looking for guidance and support from their higher power.

I can't begin to relate to you how many times I tried to stop drinking and failed. I would bet I tried to quit fifty times. My shrink told me on numerous occasions that if I didn't stop drinking, I wouldn't live to see age fifty-five, but at that point, I didn't even care! By nature, I'm a very caring person, but one of the cruelest aspects of alcohol is that it takes that caring part of us and rips it right out.

So, what if I hadn't made that fifty-first try to quit? I'd be dead! Boy, am I glad I decided to get up and try one more time. Today, I have deep-rooted resilience, and it is such a tremendous advantage for which I am grateful every day.

George Patton once said, "Success is how high you bounce after you hit bottom." Well, I'm on a bungee cord to the heavens, and I'm taking everybody I know with me. I am sitting on one sweet victory, and the opportunities my failures have awarded me are astronomical.

Openness

(This includes open-mindedness—being receptive to other arguments or ideas and open-endedness—not rigorously fixed.)

The fact that many great successes have followed and resulted from great failures has been shown to be true over and over again throughout history, but in our day-to-day routines, we tend to forget this. When we fail, we tend to think of our uniqueness, that nobody else has ever failed before. We forget that failures can sometimes catapult us to far greater heights of success than we ever dreamed. But to continue to climb to new heights, we must remain open-minded.

Take for example, Christopher Columbus, one of the most famous failures of all time. His goal was to find a 'back door' to India, where all the riches were. What a total fiasco his journey turned out to be!

The best part of this story is that by failing to reach India, Columbus achieved a far greater success—the discovery of America! But the world had to be *open-minded* enough to recognize what he had accomplished. We had to be *open-minded* to the fact that the Earth was not flat.

The same notion that we need to be open to new ideas holds true today. Alcohol drove me to the depths of despair because I wasn't *open* to recovery and its potential. I wasn't *open* to the fact that quite possibly I could live without alcohol. The first few treatment centers were *closed-minded* to the fact that I might have some underlying issues fueling my substance abuse.

Ray Kroc made eight trips to various banks before he could convince any of them to lend him money so that he could open his first McDonald's. A number of banks lost out because they were *closed-minded* to his revolutionary ideas.

To remain successful, we must consider any success as an open-ended project. It is a fluid, evolving experience, not a one-time event. By looking at it as temporary, we get a better long-range view of it. That was where I made the greatest mistake of my life. In my mid-forties, I figured I had attained all my goals. I had a beautiful boy and girl, a nice home, and I was happily married to a successful husband. I was even a good tennis player, which was very important to me at the time. By the standards I was brought up to believe in, I had done well. I had 'arrived!'

I had arrived all right, and was on the brink of complete destruction.

I had what looked like success, but I didn't have *authentic* success. Why? My thinking was closed-ended, and my life was at a dead-end. I had stopped imagining. I had stopped dreaming. I wasn't open to new challenges, new opportunities for success. Instead of regarding the satisfaction of my material desires as a means for future opportunities to extend myself and expand my options, I had gotten the end mixed up with the means. I had taken these satisfactions to be the final end and aim of life.

Resting on our laurels only leads to no more laurels. Successful people never rest, but use previous accomplishments as opportunities for further achievement. After I completed my first book, I said to myself, "Okay, I've finished that, now what?" I have learned to leave the door *open*, and listen for new thoughts. We must look at every completion as a new beginning. Cassandra Wilson, the great jazz vocalist, put it this way: "You've always got to imagine there's someplace you've got to go to. Because if you feel you're at the top, you're at the end."

Today, I continue to find experiences that push me beyond my comfort zone. I chose to write short stories while this book incubated in my brain's cul-de-sacs. Now, the question I ask myself a lot is, "What new challenge can I master?"

Compatibility

The ability to exist together in harmony.

Snowflakes are one of nature's most fragile things, but just look at what they can do when they stick together.

— Vesta M. Kelly

Synergy (synthesized energy) is the exciting concept whereby blended energies produce magnified outcomes. Snowflakes create a synergy when they come together, and we achieve our goals in direct proportion to the synergistic affiliations that we nurture.

Success is about winning professionally and personally by building up others. Success is a lifetime task of collaboration with other human beings.

Today, my associations are with people who enhance my life, and oftentimes this enhancement takes the form of me helping them. My life is decorated with good people. Ways to collect decent people include: being personable (pleasant to be around, and easy to get along with) and being able to laugh at ourselves. We must not take ourselves too seriously.

What I do is, when I meet someone, I concentrate on making them feel comfortable. In doing this, my own self-consciousness seems to melt away, which is an added benefit. That is one of the great secrets of being congenial. If people like themselves a little better when they are near us, they will love us. They will find ways to be around us. They'll seek our companionship. But how do we get people to like themselves when they are with us? By using all the attributes that make us better—being grateful, kind, patient, adaptable and willing to compromise.

The more we alter our natural self-centeredness by serving others, the more people will be drawn to us. One of the best ways to become successful is to surround ourselves with successful people. Behind every achiever is usually another achiever. No one achieves greatness without the help of others. By reaching out to others with generosity, we lay the foundation for lasting relationships.

The most powerful tool we have for building lasting and mutually beneficial relationships is a service attitude, in which our goal in every relationship is to add value to the other person's life. If we approach our relationships with that attitude, we will always be able to find shelter in the friendship and trust of others.

Steven Covey, in *The Seven Habits of Highly Effective People*, talks about 'win—win' as the frame of mind that constantly seeks mutual benefit in all human interactions. Agreements between individuals in a win—win situation are satisfying to everybody involved. One person's success is not attained at the expense of another's. Now, this is a wonderful way to interact with our fellow human beings, but we still need to check it out with God. Is it pleasing to Him?

Enthusiasm

The state of being inspired.

Enthusiasm is one of the most empowering and attractive characteristics we can have. The level of our talent isn't nearly as important as the intensity of our passion.

Nothing great was ever achieved without enthusiasm.

— Ralph Waldo Emerson

When we're excited about something, we're better able to entice others to share our passion and enthusiasm. Passion, enthusiasm, élan is contagious. When we're passionate, we're focused, purposeful, and determined, without even having to try. Without passion, we merely exist, and are reduced to mediocrity and indifference. When we're enthusiastic about something, work seems like play. We can say "I love my life" as the ultimate definition of success.

After Albert Einstein died, his brain was studied for years. Finally, the scientists were prepared to announce the results on what was different about Einstein's brain. The findings were 100% conclusive that there was absolutely nothing different about his brain. He merely took advantage of his potential to its utmost, because he loved what he was doing, and his enthusiasm never waned (*The Miracle of Change*, Wholey, p. 198).

Pursuing our passion will sustain us when no external rewards seem evident.

You have to find something that you love enough to be able to take risks, jump over the hurdles, and break through the brick walls that are always going to be placed in front of you. If you don't have that kind of feeling for what it is you're doing, you'll stop at the first giant hurdle.

— George Lucas

Make sure that the career you choose is one you enjoy. If you don't enjoy what you're doing, it will be difficult to give the extra time, effort, and devotion it takes to be a success.

— Kathy Whitworth, professional golfer

We all have layers and layers of potential, but many of us never reach our full potential because we are not doing what we love. Most of us are more prepared in and motivated by what fascinates us. Our passions tend to transcend other thoughts. We are more apt to dwell on what gives us pleasure. The chance for success at what we are passionate about is much greater than anywhere else in our lives.

When we enjoy doing something, we make it a priority. We discipline ourselves to be able to include it in our lives. We make sacrifices in other areas of our life in order to be able to concentrate on our passion. And sacrifice is usually the only difference between those who succeed and those who don't.

Self-esteem

The appreciation of one's worth.

Nothing is more important to our well-being than the opinion we have of ourselves. To value ourselves, we must first recognize, and then accept, what we can't change. Acceptance is critical. Without acceptance, we would never move forward. People with low self-esteem or self-doubt do not do well when up against *the committee.*

You know, that itty, bitty committee that lives rent-free in our brains, the one that is telling me at this very moment that "This chapter on success doesn't belong in a book on recovery. That pain in my back probably isn't just PMS cramps, because I haven't been having cramps lately. It's probably some sort of advanced cancer that has metastasized into the bones in my back, and I may only have a few weeks to live. Why then am I sitting at my computer when I could be calling my son to express my dying thoughts, since the last time I talked to him was last Wednesday, when he had a call come through and told me he'd call right back and here it is Saturday."

You're nodding now, saying 'Yes, I have an itty, bitty committee like that one.' That's the one I'm talking about. So, I'm doing my best here, and tell the little committee that I don't need its degradation, and that if it doesn't have anything nice to say about me or success, to just shut up so that I can be more productive and therefore more successful without its rude comments.

Now this is the kind of energy that needs to be captured for better use. We don't need to be filling our heads with negativity and destructive thoughts. But it takes a certain amount of self-esteem to counteract non-productive thinking, and to know that what we are doing is worthwhile. Without self-esteem, it's difficult to tap into our inner strengths. Self-esteem is a tool that can help us weather thousands of obstacles.

Another way to build our esteem is by continuously stretching to reach our full potential. Having a self-worth more powerful than any rejection or failure that we encounter enables us to move forward with confidence. With high self-esteem, it is difficult for failures to defeat us. We can accept setbacks and move on. This kind of self-worth is essential for continued success.

Spirituality
Sensitivity or attachment to a higher power.
What does spirituality have to do with success?

One of the most fundamental character traits common to all successful individuals whom I have studied, is that they all believe in God.

— Denis Waitley *(Seeds of Greatness)*

By adhering to God's principles on a daily basis, we exponentially increase our chances of success. Nothing can compare with the power derived from our trusting acceptance of His gentle perfection. On the contrary, by refusing to place God first, I am deprived of His help. The way the people in the big house around the corner from us (the Taj Mahal) made their living wasn't pleasing to God, or to the government, for that matter.

Belief in a power greater than ourselves, who I choose to call God, carries a huge amount of positives in concentrated form. Faith increases our social awareness, expanding our interest and perspective. Keeping God central in my life helps keep me from getting all mucked up in self-gratification, which is one of the core traits often found among the success-challenged. Let's look at what the Bible has to say about success.

Human effort and success must always be measured and eval-uated by what God thinks of it.

— I Corinthians 10:31

In other words, we're not a success just because we think we are. We must make our goals compatible with God *and* our fellow man. This is God's view of success. So to be truly successful, let's make it a win—win—win agreement. You plus me plus God creates infinite possibilities. The ability to continually develop win—win—win relationships both personally and professionally is a huge determinant to ongoing success.

Success is best achieved under His direction. Fulfilling our uniqueness within His moral and ethical guidelines will bring us success upon success. When we start having little victories, a momentum begins. Every success empowers us for more success. As we become more successful, we are in a position to give more and take less. All of my successes since I turned my life around are a direct result of adherence to His plan, which includes: *Persever-ance, Resilience, Openness, Compatibility, Enthusiasm, Self-es-teem and Spirituality.*

We can become all we want to be (a success) if we continually utilize all the talents of mind and spirit inherent within each of us. This ongoing process of fulfilling one's potential to the max creates happiness and contentment. It is pretty difficult to have one without the other. Authentic success goes hand in hand with happiness, which is explored in the next chapter.

Happiness, the Great Paradox of Human Nature

Entire forests have been denuded in an effort to understand the how, why, where and when of happiness. I've run across a number of definitions of this extreme state of well-being. 'A life lived in harmony with high ideals' is one. Happiness is the companion of right living. It is calm and peaceful. It cannot live in an environment of constant worry and hopeless struggle.

The word 'happiness' evokes visions of opening presents on Christmas morning, responding with unbridled laughter to a comedian's jokes, or indulging in a large spread of epicurean delights served at some exotic locale. But if happiness depends on circumstances, what happens when all the gifts have been opened, all the funny stories have been told, and we have eaten our fill? What happens when one of our loved ones dies, or our health takes a turn for the worse? If happiness depends on happenings, it will remain elusive.

Happiness, or the lack of it, quite often depends on my relationship with God and His plan for me. For me, real happiness is the joy that accompanies the quiet, confident assurance of God's love and work in my life. It is the satisfaction deep in my soul, not of my mind or body.

Personally, I've never known a spiritual person who was unhappy for very long. I know what you're saying right now. You're saying, "Oh no, please don't bore me with all that spiritual stuff again." Don't worry. I won't bore you with it. I only mention it here because it's one of the best resources for happiness.

Happiness has some clever imitators that simulate its appearance. Money can make our lifestyle easier. We can buy pleasure, we can acquire 'things.' But money is neither inherently good nor inherently bad. It is our reaction to it that determines whether it will be a positive or a negative in our lives.

The almighty greenback won't make us happy, but neither will not having any. A significant increase in the financial resources available to us can be tricky. Expanding our number of options can be a disruption in our lives, and even lead us astray. Research conducted recently at the University of Missouri at Columbia asked college students from the United States and South Korea what made them happy. The results showed that money was far down on the list.

Happiness can coexist with poverty, tribulation or sorrow, making it one of the great paradoxes of nature. It can live under any circumstances, thrive under any conditions.

In the Bible, the Book of Philippians is Paul's letter of joy. Those unfamiliar with the Bible wouldn't guess that Paul wrote this lighthearted letter from, of all places, prison. How was it possible for him to be happy under the most deplorable conditions of confinement? Paul found happiness by consistently focusing on God.

When we look at the happiest people we know, the people with the most positive, energized attitudes in our office, in our family, and in our community, it's highly likely that they have two things in common. They may be from different cultures, and in different stages of their careers, but these positively charged people are working toward goals (their purpose) while doing what they love to do (their passion).

Another paradox is that the basis of true happiness is always found in the love of something outside of ourselves. It is the love of mankind—be it between a man and a woman, or parent and child, or the love of our lifework to which we devote all our energies. There is a certain spiritual joy associated with overcoming a bad habit or rising above an inner struggle. I have found it spiritually uplifting to turn away from the groveling material side of life. Only recently have I begun to do this, but I have experienced a tremendous sense of freedom by not always wanting 'things.'

Following a recent study, Kennon M. Sheldon reported the following conclusions in the *Journal of Personality and Social Psychology*: the top four things that made the participants in the survey happiest were—autonomy (feeling that our activities are self-chosen and self-endorsed), competence (feeling that we are effective in our activities), relatedness (feeling a sense of closeness with others) and finally, self-esteem.

Gratification (a harmony between our desires and our possessions) can be an element of happiness, but let's take eating, for example. After we've eaten, we're full, and have lost our desire to eat. Therefore, for the moment, eating can no longer gratify us. The pleasure is only temporary, and cannot give us sustained happiness.

Contentment is Overrated

In actuality, real happiness is a rare emotion, seldom experienced on a continuing basis. Absolute, perfect, continuous happiness in life isn't going to happen. We must take that fact and, joyfully or not so joyfully, adjust to it. It is part of living.

The ebb and flow of happiness is part of the natural cycle of things. It is an extreme state. Knowing this, it is easier to accept pain knowing that happiness will return. At times, we will become content or satiated, but God made human nature's former state of dissatisfaction the one to which we will always revert.

It is our nature to return to a state of want or need. This indestructible force of nature enables us to survive. If we didn't become hungry again, we would stop eating and die. Since we cannot change the way our bodies naturally function, we must accept this restless default state in order to use it for what it is meant to be—an advantage.

Dissatisfaction can be a huge advantage. We wouldn't grow, have new ambitions, or be open to new ideas if we resided in an eternal state of satisfaction. Ongoing complacency deadens our desire to rise to higher levels of growth, but it works well if we consider it as merely an interval, a respite before we move on to higher levels of accomplishment.

We should always try to look at life as if we are just starting out. We must never look at ourselves as 'having it made.' Contentment is great at the end of our day's activities when it is important to slow down, but we should never consider it a goal or destination, but merely a resting point following the completion of another step.

Dr. Joyce Brothers, one of the world's leading psychologists, states that true happiness has to do with its frequency, not its intensity. Good news, like finding the person with whom we want to spend the rest of our life, makes us blissful for a while. But when we become accustomed to that person being around, our initial state of ecstasy subsides. Most things lose their fascination after we've acquired them.

On the flip side, we may experience a debilitating accident or illness, and sink into a deep depression. This is a critical time, when we either decide to move on to lead a happy life, regardless of our physical restrictions, or we become stagnant and bitter.

I have never seen Bill angrier than immediately after his massive stroke, when he began to understand the profound gravity of his condition. I remember him yelling and screaming at the team of doctors when they told him that he would only regain minimal use of the right side of his body. On that day, I'm sure that he felt he would never, ever have another 'happy' day in his life.

Fast-forward to many years later, and we cannot begin to count the joy-filled days we have had, and continue to have, together. Hundreds of times he's had to wipe his eyes with his sleeve because he was laughing so hard that a stream of tears had flooded his face.

How do we regain happiness after a great sadness, sorrow, or calamity in our life? First, we must grieve. There are specific stages of grief, with the last one being acceptance. Only through acceptance can happiness return. Acceptance is critical. Bill had to accept his limitations, and I had to accept mine, before we could move forward. Acceptance is the gateway to recovery. It opens the way for us to grow. With acceptance comes wisdom. And wisdom promotes happiness.

Just as everybody has a natural point at which their body weight tends to settle, studies show that our disposition has its own natural point toward which our temperament gravitates. Our happiness level is heavily weighted by heredity, but there are ways to elevate our natural standard of comfort.

Delayed Gratification will Significantly Improve our Chances for Happiness

Many persons have the wrong idea about what constitutes true happiness. It is not attained through self-gratification but through fidelity to a worthy purpose.

— Helen Keller

Delayed gratification, the ability to sacrifice what we want now for what we want later, can produce great rewards. Delayed gratification simply means being able to resist the urge for immediate pleasure, and instead choose the course of action that will pay off later. Delaying gratification is a process of scheduling the pain and enjoyment in life in such a way as to enhance future rewards by meeting and experiencing the pain first, and getting past it. It is the ability to subordinate an impulse for a far *greater* but *later* reward. It takes a certain amount of maturity, which includes basing a judgment on the big picture, the long haul.

Caffeine, nicotine, alcohol, compulsive sex, gambling, overeating, and prescription drugs (just to name a few) produce instant gratification for many, but are counterproductive. They are quick to reward, but difficult to quit. They can be habit-forming and very addictive for some people. The need for instant gratification is the root cause of today's epidemic of chemical dependency. When we quit this stuff, we delay a small, quick impulse, but this can vastly improve our lives.

Delayed gratification increases our quality of life. Let me explain why. When we anticipate the occurrence of a probable future event (one we desire), our current perceived well-being is immediately raised. This means that we could be doing something we dislike at the time, but since we are looking forward to something we enjoy, we feel better about our situation, and about our life as a whole. We get to enjoy the anticipation along with the actual event. Anticipation is a pleasure that we deny when we go for immediate gratification.

Finally, when enjoying the much-anticipated activity, we don't have to think about the undesirable task, because it's already been completed. The extension of our improved sense of well-being affords us the opportunity for still greater fulfillment, because we reap a double blessing. Simple idea, right? But so many people refuse to live this way. They want everything now. But by having it now, they miss out on half the enjoyment! If we want to be happier, we must know our responsibilities, and schedule our pleasures around them. We must not plan our fun before we think about our work.

According to M. Scott Peck in *The Road Less Traveled*, the bestseller that sold millions and was translated into many languages, delaying gratification for the *later* but *greater* reward is the only decent way to live.

No Matter Where We Go, There We Are

Today, I make my happiness a priority, because I'm no good to anyone else if I'm feeling out of sorts. Think of the message flight attendants always announce right before take off. "Make sure your oxygen mask is securely fastened before attempting to help someone else." This same principle applies to the way we live. We must take care of ourselves before we can be of service to others.

Taking care of ourselves can start with the little things. If I'm not in the mood to clean up the breakfast dishes right away, I rinse them and write for an hour. I can guarantee you that after an hour at my computer, washing dishes serves as a nice little break, and no harm was done in the process.

Today, I know that if something doesn't get done immediately, chances are there's a good reason for the postponement of the task, and it will probably get done later. I no longer let my 'to do' lists mess with me. Lists are excellent tools to get us organized, but they don't have to become a dictatorship. If we don't complete our 'to do' list today, we've got tomorrow's list already made.

Part of happiness is learning to enjoy the lulls, for they will always be there, no matter where we are on our journey. Happiness abides in the small things in life, and in taking the time to enjoy them. Happiness is found in striving toward a goal, rather than the attainment of it. The glory that follows victory is brief, only fleeting moments anyway. Only by being productively active can I feel my best. It's the day-to-day work on this book that brings me great pleasure. A forty-five minute walk revitalizes me, and increases my capacity for contentment for the rest of the day.

I find that diversification helps me to relax, and enjoy the transition of body and spirit. Going from one major satisfying project to another is deeply gratifying.

The only drawback is that it sometimes drives my husband crazy. I've got more gratifying projects waiting in every available nook and cranny. Bill's finally come to terms with the fact that in that particular area, any improvement may be marginal.

Purpose can ignite your spirit, providing personal meaning and deep satisfaction to your life. Purpose is the why—why you are here—and your own special calling. Purpose is the unique gifts and insights that you bring to the planet and can contribute to your world. Purpose fuels your efforts and gives you the drive to continue, no matter what the challenges.

— Cynthia Kersey (*Unstoppable*)

The best resource we have for happiness is our passion. When we choose to do what really matters to us, there is less of a struggle, and a natural driving force takes over, making it easier for us to fulfill our potential. Our passion enlivens and reengages our hearts.

When we're excited about something, we become very creative. Creativity is one of those tools necessary to help us solve our most difficult problems. Creativity produces positive feelings of engagement and hope. It is necessary in our response to hardship.

So, what exactly is creativity? It is simply the process of exploring the unknown; the mental capacity to make something new again. During the act of creating, we are focused, energy is released, and our life has meaning. When our creations give others pleasure, we have the added benefit of impacting others.

One of the complex abilities with which our human race is blessed is a creative imagination. It enables us to dream, which lends direction to our lives. Since we operate in ever-changing environments, we must be creative to continually adjust to the diverse landscapes that appear before us. The life maps and charts that we have *devised* need to be continually *revised*.

To plan, we must first be able to imagine, to visualize. Visualization is a form of constructive daydreaming. All world-class athletes and other peak performers visualize. By replaying past victories, success becomes ingrained in our memory, and becomes a natural reflex.

One of the most durable satisfactions in life is to lose oneself in one's work.

— Harry E. Fordick

When we are in our bliss, we are in a state of effortless action in which we and our project become one. This total engagement is another road toward fulfillment. We will never be happy by being busy for the sake of it, but we'll find joy by getting involved with things that energize us (what we're avid about). For me, writing is a clever passport to powerful insight and observation by which I truly learn to appreciate like never before everything from a paper clip to the Sistine Chapel.

The process of finding our passion can be daunting, but it can also be extremely rewarding. One of the interests I pursued when I first got into recovery was drawing. I gave it a good try, but soon discovered that my talent wasn't far above smiley faces and stick figures. At the time, I was frustrated, but my growth as an individual depended upon this healthy process of trial and error. I have a good friend in recovery who tried writing before he found his true passion to be painting. So, we all must experiment in order to find out what gives us the most satisfaction.

When I was child, I was asked countless times, "What do you want to be when you grow up?" Later on, as a young adult the question was asked with more urgency, but never once was my answer, "A writer, I want a career in writing." Back then, "bodybuilding" had a better chance of being my answer.

In high school, I excelled in math, and was encouraged to go into business. Mom figured that it was the quickest way to build wealth. She had been without money most of her life, and she wanted her kids to have a better life. My parents let it be known that they would pay for my college education on one condition—I had to major in business. On that issue, there would be no compromise. I didn't know what I wanted to do, and who I wanted to be, so I was grateful for a push in any direction.

For me, writing was a necessity to get through school, college and postgraduate work. It served me well. After graduating magna cum laude in business administration, I quickly retired my rhetoric to letters and the email portion of my online activities. The thought never trickled through my cluttered mind that one day, writing would have a profound impact, changing the rest of my life.

After college, I went into sales and job-hopped, seeking the one product that would brighten my and everyone else's life. I soon found that it wasn't the merchandise that disillusioned me. I was disturbed by the whole business of persuading people into buying arbitrary things, especially products they didn't need or want. Suffering from a bad case of social phobia didn't help my selling performance, either. Sales wasn't for me, but I pressed on, with my friend alcohol close by my side. I sold items from lipstick to laxatives, thinking that one day, my struggles would pay off.

While trying to find satisfaction in my employment, my husband and I met with debilitating illnesses, one right after the other, rocking both of us and our loved ones to our inner sanctums. As I've mentioned before, Bill had a brain hemorrhage, and by then I had been struggling with alcoholism for a number of years. Endless anger engulfed me, mingling with the bitter aftertaste of fear— fear that life as I knew it was over. I had a terrible time making any sense of all the destruction in our lives, but I had to change, or else I would die.

For months, our family searched for answers, our faith helping more than anything. In my effort to find comfort, I took someone's advice and began journaling.

It was also recommended in rehab. The idea was to write about everyday events, and my corresponding feelings. That way, I would also have a record of what triggered good days, and what set me back a little.

I started this assignment not liking it at all, but I wanted to feel better, and so I approached it much like I did schoolwork—an essential evil. After all, I was now a student determined to learn how to make the best of the rest of my life. This tedious journaling exercise went on for months, but in the meantime I noticed something happening. Along with my hurt feelings, I began to jot down neat little word formations about people, places and things, and I found myself enjoying this creative process.

With a lot of free time on my hands, I also began reading extensively. There was a small library at Rancho L'Abri, the rehab center I was confined to, with mostly books focusing on recovery, but I could only read those for so long.

Pleasure could still play a big part in my life, although no one would have convinced me of this at the time, so I picked up a copy of *Sophie's Choice* by William Styron. I related to the story, because Sophie was also battling demons—many not of her making. Not only was I captivated by the story, but it got me out of myself and my own problems. I loved the way Styron wrote. I marked pages I particularly liked so that I could read them again later. I learned that I loved the sensuality of words, the joy of ideas.

Gradually, I became more observant, more aware of my surroundings. I found myself lying awake at night, wondering about the excitement in my life. People were captivating my attention. I discovered they were multi-dimensional, more complex than I ever remembered them being. At routine events, I was no longer bored. I was too busy looking for fun observations to spit back out on paper. Even journaling turned out to be a very rewarding experience, in that it taught me to look at myself on a daily basis and ask, "How am I doing?"

I began to realize that I had in my life experienced situations the average person would never encounter. A lot of interesting things had happened to me. Maybe I could put these together in the form of a story. How many people have been locked down in a psychiatric ward (not that it's anything to be proud of) or been sent away for months (not that that's anything to be proud of either) just to learn how to do life without destroying myself and everybody else around me.

The places where I had been confined aren't usually found on many 'Exotic places to see' lists. Most people don't wake up one morning and say "Oh, what a beautiful morning. I think I'll check myself into rehab!" When a bunch of drunks, pill heads, junkies, and speed freaks are thrown together for any length of time, I assure you all bets are off. Some of the personal stories I listened to in rehab made *Leaving Las Vegas* look like a Disney flick. Soon, my fiddling with pen, paper and processor began to take the form of a story, with characters evolving from people I knew. Something else was happening, too. I was beginning to think less about myself.

In the past, whenever I had attempted to sober up, I had always panicked. What was I going to do with all my free time? Life was so boring. Drinking always took care of that. But I couldn't drink anymore. Well, I could, but…well, we won't go there. Too many people told me that if I continued to drink, I would die. All those people couldn't be wrong. Maybe, just maybe, they were right.

So I was uncomfortable for a while. I learned that it's okay to feel uncomfortable, and that we almost always live through it. Besides, it can be a good growth place. I had been humbled; I was teachable. To fill up my time, I started to play tennis again. I also went to a lot of 12-step meetings, to church, and began walking and going to the gym. My life also included movies, good food, reading and yes, writing. I was developing good habits. I was taking care of myself.

Today, I like the suspense of not knowing what's around the next corner. This is what gives life its true zest. As Chuck C. says in *A New Pair of Glasses*, it isn't what we know that makes life interesting, it's what we don't know. Today, my life may take a significant turn, and all I did was get up and show up.

As a result of a series of devastating setbacks, I had found a new life skill. I also realized that down the road, my writing could be used as an encouragement. Uncovering layers of emotion, I stumbled upon one of my life's passions. Maybe I had even found an obscure reason for the tragic events in my life.

Writing has helped me out of my worst despair, and has brought a new dimension to my existence. One supreme joy for me is encountering new knowledge, and I do that daily through reading and writing. Today, I depend on writing when I need to get out of myself, and even when I don't.

Another one of my passions, having been given this great gift of life, is to help others find the fulfillment that has freely been given me. I have great dreams, and try to do at least one thing toward them every day. And I dream big, because I know that I will never attain anything higher than the highest target in my dearest dreams.

Happiness is a by-product of setting goals, attaining them, setting new ones, and on and on. It sneaks up on those of us who work hard at pursuing our dreams. What a nice bonus. We are so busy doing what we love to do that we don't have to worry about finding happiness.

One of the most important literary figures of the 1900s, once said:

This is the true joy in life—that being used for a purpose recognized by yourself as a mighty one. That being a force of nature, instead of a feverish, selfish little clod of ailments and grievances, claiming that the world will not devote itself to making you happy.

— George Bernard Shaw

Our Bodies' Health is the Foundation of our Happiness

Vibrant health is the kind of health that makes one feel literally intoxicated with life, with the urge to do and be beyond the capacity and limitations of any day's efforts, with untiring energy, clarity of mind, and unquenchable enthusiasm.

— Dr. Norman Walker

Wouldn't it be fabulous to live every waking moment experiencing vibrant health? This is not possible, but there are ways to increase the frequency of feeling vibrantly alive.

Our physical dimension is our vehicle to get us through life. If we take care of our bodies, they will support our efforts to be all we were meant to be.

Health is not only to be well—but to use well—every power we have.

— Florence Nightingale

Vibrant health is about embracing life, not just avoiding death. And if we don't take care of our bodies and our minds, they won't be able to provide us with the energy and intellect required to be successful and productive.

When health is absent, wisdom cannot reveal itself, art cannot become manifest, strength cannot be exerted, wealth is useless and reason is powerless.

— Herophilies

The Grateful Head

Gratitude is essentially a spiritual appreciation for our life within, around and beyond us. It is a quick and easy way to become positive and feel secure, providing us with one of the widest roads to happiness. This thankful state is sometimes hard for people to embrace, because they feel overwhelmed by all their problems, but there are ways to rise from the burial grounds of the grateful dead. This is important, because when we are grateful for what we have, our happiness factor increases by 200%.

If we dwell on what we don't have, we're going to feel bad. If we dwell on what we do have, we will feel good. It's that simple. Just like so many of our assets, our gratitude needs to be continually exercised to help it keep growing, to keep it from atrophying.

The more I express my gratitude, the more things I find for which to be thankful. When I'm concentrating on my good fortune, it is pretty hard to feel sorry for myself.

Many of us keep gratitude lists. This is a concrete way to enumerate and appreciate all the wonderful things in our life. If we make one, we'll want to keep it handy, since it is a quick and easy reminder of our blessings. If it is close by, it will also be convenient to add things, as we surely will. This gratitude regimen builds our stamina for appreciation.

To help separate their blessings from their troubles, some people keep God boxes. That's where they put their prayers and wishes, and anything they feel would be better left in God's capable hands. This tangible way of dumping troubles makes it easy for someone who just can't seem to appreciate good fortune. One of my friends has two God boxes. One is gold, and one is black. The gold one is for blessings, and for answered prayers. The black one is for her worries and disappointments. These she has turned over to God. That box is very light, not because she hasn't seen heartache, but because they're God's worries, not hers.

Here, there is at least visible evidence of 'turning it over.' Every time her problems start creeping back into her thoughts, she can consciously say, "No, I've given them to God." Turning our troubles over to God can release us from their burden, and open the door to thanksgiving.

There are clearly events in my life that I should regret, but I am eternally grateful for having battled them. I've learned to feel gratitude instead of disappointment, making my life richer and happier. The internal wars I had to overcome have made me who I am today and although those wars were at times very painful, they have made me stronger and wiser.

Whether we believe in the Koran or the Talmud, in Lao-tzu or the Bible, in the Sanskrit Proverb or a spiritual 12-step program (there are many other religions, too many to list here), the universal spiritual themes contained in each of these contribute immensely to joy and happiness.

The search for happiness is the search for God, although very few people understand this great truth.
— Elinor MacDonald

My beliefs bring me pure joy every second I'm awake, and peace of mind as I fall asleep at night. To me, happiness is to be secure enough to develop a hunger to give. And I give by sharing what happened to me, and how I survived life's most profound calamities. It includes sorrows outlived, and pain resolved by the wisdom of years, that translates my suffering and loss into love and empathy for others.

I am forever thankful that I have turned my will and my life over to His care. He offers much-needed direction and, even when I fall short of the mark, He still loves me just the same. That is the 'grace' we are all given. We are part of His greater plan, and He is using us for His purpose.

Here in America, we have so many reasons to be grateful. Shortly after 9/11, I automatically began feeling gratitude. Now, this didn't happen on day one or day two. I had to work through my fears first. But I soon began to feel grateful that the hijacked planes weren't completely filled with people; that one of the planes didn't hit the White House. I had gratitude for the heroes on the plane that crashed in Pennsylvania, and for the workers on the ground.

I had this gratitude because I knew God would make things good again. I knew that God would turn the horrible ugliness into something beautiful. One of the worst things to ever happen to America has brought out the very best in every single one of us. Nothing has been more beautiful than the hands of America reaching out to help one another with an even stronger commitment to freedom and unity. On the blackest of days, no amount of fire, smoke or terror could match the courage of rescue workers and ordinary citizens who risked their lives to save others who were in danger. And then, turning bad things into good things was witnessed again in my community as we all rushed to the aid of the Katrina victims.

How did I know that God would turn these horrible tragedies into something good? He has demonstrated His awesome power to transform negative events over and over again, in my life and in the lives of countless others. He has taken every destructive experience I've ever had and is using it for much greater good. Clearly, the greatest single event in my life happened when the combination of my triple whammy nearly beat me to death. He took what might have destroyed me and used it to transform me, and as many people as I can reach out to with my story.

So Grateful for that Second Chance

He has added grace upon grace in my life. When my lifelong depression and other bothersome conditions that I had struggled with my entire life were finally brought under control, many of my fears disappeared right along with them. I rebuilt my relationship with my husband and children, and our love today is greater than it's ever been.

Off in the shoulder of life's normal path, I learned a design for living I wouldn't have found anywhere else. I have learned more in recovery than I did in the previous forty-five years, even though the previous forty-five included completion of grade school, high school and college.

With gratitude, I like to think that I have been given two lives —the one I learned with, and the one I'm living now. A young man, just twenty-three years of age, in one of my 12-step meetings, explained it this way: "You know when you go to an ophthalmologist and he's adjusting the various lenses in front of your face until he gets you the perfect prescription? While he flips the lenses into place in front of your eyes, he asks you, 'Is it better this way, or this way? This way, or here?' Well, he can stop flipping. It's definitely better this way. I've found my prescription for life."

These words came from Kevin, who had had his back broken by a bunch of gang members. He will be in constant pain for the rest of his life, and has to stand in our meetings, because it's too painful for him to sit down. Yet, he is one of the most grateful people I know.

At many 12-step meetings, we are given a list of topics to choose from to lend direction to the meeting. The subject that is chosen helps us stay focused. Of all the topics available, gratitude is one of the most popular subjects. Since there are twelve months in a year, in Southern California we tend to emphasize the step that corresponds with the month. January is the first step, etc. The eleventh step deals with gratitude; therefore, November is gratitude month, and what better month than the month of Thanksgiving. Gratitude is so important to recovery that we devote an entire month to it!

The way a lot of us look at it is if we hadn't experienced such debilitating setbacks, we would never have learned a way of life that leads us from despair. We have been given the opportunity to experience a profound transformation that other people never have a chance to undergo. It is a way of life not taught in schools or churches per se, and certainly one I never learned until now.

When I talk about my husband recovering from a massive stroke, you'll notice I don't say that he is still suffering the effects, and how miserable he is. He has more gratitude today than he has ever had in his entire life. The major reason for his gratefulness? He is a God-centered man now. It took a brain hemorrhage for God to get his attention, but we are grateful He did.

Ever since college, Bill had been running, running, running. Busy, busy, busy. To a certain degree this was okay, but there was no balance in his life. The mental dimension of his life took up 40%, and the physical aspect of his life took up another 40%. That left 19% for his emotions and 1% (if that) for any spirituality. Today, the four dimensions that make up his life are more equally divided.

For me, life is a process of uncovering, discovering, and discarding, but I know that somewhere along the way, there will be trouble. These future challenges will once again be opportunities for gratitude instead of self-pity. Gratitude may not be immediate, but I can take comfort knowing that it will eventually return.

We all deserve to be happy, but if we harbor bitterness, happiness will dock elsewhere. We all have our mountains, and they all need to be climbed. But the good news is that most of the happiness is found during the climb...not at the top. The more we pay attention to our health, our relationships, the quality of our work and the balance of play, the happier we will be.

The time to be happy is now. The way to be happy is to make others so.

— Robert G. Ingersoll

Our Bonus Age

For many years, it was popular to believe that age 65 was the point where active life ended and old age began. Today, people are moving past this arbitrary retirement age by starting second careers, taking up new interests and staying active physically. We are breaking out of old stereotypes and reinventing ourselves, not just once, but over and over again.

Today is the best time in history to be getting older. Modern medicine and ongoing medical breakthroughs, along with improved lifestyles, continue to extend the lifespan of humans. Scientists predict that new technologies will add decades or more to the average person's lifetime.

Society's realization of the potential productivity available to us in our later years has caused us to rethink the term 'old age.' Now, there is youth, and middle age, but not old age anymore. New terms such as our third age, the age of mastery, or our second adulthood, have come into vogue. These concepts are based on the belief that as we age, we are merely moving from one stage of our lives to another, with declines, but also with advances. It is our responsibility to recognize the unique rewards of each. These are gifts which belong solely to us.

The Baby Boomer generation, by its sheer size, has reconfigured the way society looks at aging. Along with living longer and healthier lives, we've added new words to our vocabulary. During the 1990s, the term 'gerontologist' was coined. Gerontologists are specialists who study the biological, psychological, and sociological phenomena associated with aging. Gerontologists came up with the term 'third age.' Gail Sheehy, author of the classic best seller *Passages* and the groundbreaking *Sex and the Seasoned Woman*, has referred to this stage in our lives as the 'Second Adulthood' or the 'Age of Mastery.'

I like to think of it as our 'bonus age.' It is an age that generations before us have never lived long enough to experience. Several hundred years ago, colonial folk could only expect to live into their 30s. Today, the adult life cycle has become elongated. We can expect to live much longer than our ancestors.

For the sake of continuity however, I'll use the more common term 'third age' from this point forward. Our third age is a lot like our childhood and middle years. There is humor and sadness, but also courage, faith and hope. There is progress, but it's not necessarily the kind we can see. It's easy to be aware of the physical losses of aging, but sometimes it's more difficult to cherish or even recognize the accumulation of great mental, emotional and spiritual growth.

A couple of weeks ago, a beautiful young girl sat in front of me during one of the frequent community college classes I enjoy, and I was reminded of myself as a teen. With her deep-set eyes and long blonde hair, she captivated everybody's attention in the packed lecture hall. Her gleaming complexion revealed not a blemish. When she seductively crossed her legs, the young man next to me knocked his water bottle over, splashing us both.

As I sat there drying myself off, two people came to mind; who I was then, and who I am now. When I was her age, I had no concept of where I wanted to go, or what I wanted to do. Not everybody is like this, but I certainly was.

Don't get me wrong, I'm not putting down all the young, sexy girls who thrive on attention. This is necessary at their stage in life for, yes, their biological clocks are a tickin'. If girls didn't look attractive, what would happen to humanity? How would the human race survive? But during adolescence, my outward appearance was such a critical aspect of my self-esteem that I tended to ignore all my other assets. Being preoccupied with my looks left me with little energy to explore other innate gifts or talents. During my teens, I would not live up to my full potential, nor would I feel fulfilled.

But our youth is really the perfect time to start preparing for our bonus age. We must start early in life in order to minimize the dreaded manifestations of aging. We can't wait until we retire to start exercising, watching what we eat and exploring what makes us 'us.'

By honing our personal skills early in life, we can make our later years better. Then, by the time we hit our third age, many of us will have acquired multiple talents, so as to be flexible enough to perform, or even excel, in multiple fields of endeavor. Having these skill sets, we can be assured that if one area of our life falls apart, we have backup choices and other alternatives.

As human beings, we are all multifaceted. My physical being is only one of the four dimensions of 'me.' Today, I have an awareness that focuses on my entire being. Being less concerned with my looks leaves my mind available for other adventures. My emotional, mental and spiritual facets have taken over, as if to compensate for my now less important physical attributes.

Somewhere Between "To Hold it in" or "To Heck with it"

Did the beautiful girl in my class ever wonder what she would be like at age 50, 60, or even 70? Had she thought about how her physical beauty would diminish with time? I know I did, but what I didn't know was that it would be all right; that my inner compensation would be well worth any outward loss.

This was an epiphany for me.

While I admired this young girl, I was amazed that I was without a skerrick of envy. There was no nostril-flaring jealousy. I had always thought that being caught at this stage of my life observing some sweet young thing strut her stuff, I'd turn green enough to grow roots. But I was wrong. I was enjoying myself, with no sorrow involved. As I sat there in the classroom, there was no pull to be like her. I had already enjoyed that time in my life.

Sure, I still like to look nice. We are all works of God, and we need to respect what he has given us, but what a freedom! I was no longer defined by my body, nor enslaved by it.

I thought about everything that had happened since my adolescence: how I'd grown; how I was no longer insecure; how my self-worth had ripened and expanded; how I had developed mastery over my emotions, my environment, and my body. I'd become more focused, more goal-oriented. I didn't *have* to please everybody at this wonderful stage of my life.

One of the lessons I learned from many years of living was that the inner me is much more important *in the grand scheme of things* than any outward effects. It took time, but I have now agreed to the loss of my youth, and moved on. If there is ever an area in our lives where acceptance is invaluable, it is when we begin to grow older.

I sat there empowered by the wisdom (what we need to know to live well) given to me through years of failure and triumph. Wisdom only came to me through age and effort. There were no shortcuts. The accumulation of life experiences is a definite advantage that I gratefully acknowledge and welcome. I am now, probably for the first time in my life, the person I have always wanted to be.

Wisdom is necessary to cope with problems, avoid dangers and better manage our lives. It promotes happiness. Wisdom is not just knowing fundamental truths. Knowing about the origin of the universe doesn't make us wise if it doesn't provide us with any insight into our role and place within it. If information does not guide us, or give us a good perspective on the meaning of life, then it doesn't offer wisdom. To be wise, we must not only have knowledge and understanding, but we must also be able to use it and live it.

Maybe it's because I now have a better idea as to why I'm here that I feel so good about this stage of my life. Having triumphed over all kinds of vicissitudes, disappointments, trials and illnesses affords me a certain sense of self, security and empowerment. It is my choice as to whether I will continue to grow from setbacks, or let them devour me, but chances are I'll continue to grow, because I know that within every bad situation, there is a blessing. All I have to do is find it.

Everyone Would Like to Live a Long Life, but No One Wants to be Old

One unwished-for downside of this third age is that somewhere along the path of aging lies a minefield of possible physical ailments. Loss of our physical health and independence is one of the most traumatic issues of aging. This is like a death sentence to many, but it doesn't need to be.

As we age, our body becomes less useful, less enjoyable. During our third age, we tend to dwell on our losses mainly because they are problems that require our attention, but our physical life narrows because it is becoming less and less important.

The spiritual eyesight improves as the physical eyesight declines.

— Plato

In small ways, our bodies repeatedly prepare us for the inevitable. By the time it's time to pass on, we are much more okay with leaving our bodies behind. Unlike our flesh, our spirit does not decay with the passage of time.

It turns out that the whole journey of aging is something designed to lead us from thinking of ourselves as egos to knowing ourselves as souls. We're given opportunity after opportunity to practice letting go and to shift our perspective from ego to soul-view.

— Ram Dass *(Aging Body, Ageless Soul)*

Aging is an interesting predicament. To our egos, our physical declines are scary. Aging reminds us of our lack of control of our universe, devastating our ego. But we can solve this problem by changing our perspective (see the chapter *How am I doing as a Human Being?*). We can switch from the ego's viewpoint to the soul's perspective. With the ego's perspective, we get caught up with all our fears and dramas. From the soul's point of view, we are not emotionally caught up in any losses. The soul is sitting back 'enjoying the show.'

As we can see, the situation doesn't change, but our experience of it does. Looking at our lives from the soul's perspective doesn't just help us deal with change more effectively—this viewpoint takes us outside ourselves, to a higher vantage point.

During our third age, the idea of departing this world shifts from being an abstract recognition to an everyday awareness. It becomes more and more a reality. Our lives come into sharper focus. It's natural for us to become interested in our mortality, but we can use this fascination to our advantage. With the constant awareness of the limit on our time, we can be guided to make the very best use of it, and to live life to its fullest.

Acknowledgment of death can be an enormous asset in our life. It adds urgency. We are then more apt to search for meaningfulness. This search becomes more universal as we age. Fewer demands frees us to explore life's most important questions. I know I'm not going to live forever, but while I'm here, I'm not going to waste time lamenting what could have been, or worrying about what will be. Some people begin their spiritual quest, while others become more spiritually mature. This is one of the greatest gifts of aging. We naturally tend to grow more spiritual, from sheer terror, if nothing else.

There are no easy cures for the losses incurred in the aging process, but we can't let ourselves be defeated by them. We must not let ourselves get caught up in the mundane minutia of aging, for then we will fail to recognize new joys, challenges, and opportunities. When God closes a door (our body's effectiveness), why waist precious time dwelling on it?

Look for That Open Window

One of the most devastating elements in humanity's makeup is the urge to give up. But when defeated by the aging process, we close our life to infinite possibilities.

There are great benefits to aging, and this is where our focus should be. Studies have shown the older we get, the stronger is our sense of well-being. There are very few societal demands at this stage of our life. There is no pressure to marry, to have children, or to find an ideal career. We have already chosen a profession and earned a living. We've raised families. Our social roles are more relaxed, making our lifestyle less rigid, and much more flexible. We don't have to make long-range plans; we can enjoy life as it unfolds.

In many ways, I'm not limited by old age, but liberated by it. Today, it takes less to make me happy. It is easier for me to be positive, but up until now, I would have guessed the reverse to be true. I have more time to do what I really want. I can now concentrate (if I want) on the underdeveloped areas of my life. I'm not consumed anymore by what people think, but instead feel a great sense of serenity and tranquility. Never in all my imaginings did I think that I would feel this good as a woman over fifty years of age.

Another advantage of growing older is that many of our problems have already been solved. We've survived youth, middle age, illness, infection and diseases. Due to our wealth of experience, not only does our judgment and reasoning improve, but so do our strategies in tackling tough problems. If we hang on to our youthful sense of wonder, and add to it our wisdom from experience, the combination will serve us well. If we've learned our lessons, there are very few things left to learn the hard way.

Twentieth-century American psychoanalyst Erik Erikson introduced the concept of 'generativity,' which is a popular word among gerontologists today. This term means continuing to contribute to the next generation by performing meaningful work, creative activities, and/or staying connected to family, as opposed to becoming stagnant, inactive and quite possibly cynical as well.

Our ability to live with vitality and a sense of adventure, to stay productive and continue contributing something of value to the world, allows us to set a positive example to others who follow. It also means leaving a social legacy, which can have profound significance for generations to come.

In life, there will always be trade-offs, compromises and concessions. The privilege of having a long life is tempered by our older minds and bodies. During our third age, we will usually suffer some loss of memory, but our creative imagination is ageless. Our mental efficiency declines, but we develop better insight and perspective.

Regardless of our losses, in order to remain in the game of life, we must continue to play the various hands we are dealt, and adapt to them. Older people who are unwilling to risk suffering, changing, growing and learning are choosing the path to senility, and the rest of the world will leave them behind.

Another interesting fact about this bonus age is that as we grow older, our biological aging slows down. That's right! In other words, the more years we accumulate, the slower our body ages. Physically, we don't change as much from age 55 to 75 as we did from age 35 to 55.

Since we age at different rates, our chronological age doesn't really tell people much about us. I know old people who are thirty-five, and young people who are seventy-five. Not only do people age at different rates, but various parts of our bodies age at different rates. Our eyes begin to decline at age 10, but our muscular strength doesn't pass its peak until around age 30. For these reasons, people in their third age (more than any other age) can not be stereotyped. We are a diverse population.

Living Younger Longer

One formula for staying young is to focus on the positives in our life. We can concentrate on the parts of us that are still young, active and growing. One of these parts is our brain. Yes, you read it right—our brain. News about the aging brain is not all doom and gloom.

Our intellects are packed with expert information. We have all this knowledge we have accumulated over a lifetime. This 'crystallized intelligence,' commonly called wisdom, is a tremendous, awesome resource.

Another critical part of the 'staying young recipe' is a commitment to exercise. Everywhere we look, we are told to exercise, but I would be remiss if I did not include yet another reminder.

Regular physical activity is probably as close to a magic bullet as we will come in modern medicine.

— Dr. JoAnn Manson, Harvard's Brigham and Women's Hospital

Many of the conditions we associate with aging, such as osteoporosis, weight gain and generalized weakness, are more closely linked with loss of muscle mass due to an inactive lifestyle than the passage of years.

Exercise has a salubrious effect on our cardiovascular system. Regardless of age, people who exercise have less hardening of their arteries than people who are inactive. Exercise increases blood circulation, and the increased oxygen supply sweeps away stagnant toxic impurities.

A chronic weariness descends over our life when too little blood is pumped through our body. This sluggishness is due to the accumulation of poisonous waste products in our body's cells. By increasing the blood purifying capacity of the lungs, every cell benefits by the unclogging of these life-giving channels of energy.

Dr. Herbert de Vries, a renowned exercise physiologist from the University of Southern California, concluded from dozens of studies that regular physical activity could take 20 years off the chronological age of a once-sedentary person. His research showed that every system in the body, from the brain to the feet, could be rejuvenated by regular exercise.

Physical activity confers many benefits on the mind, as well as the body, with profound effects on our intellect, memory and emotions. Dr. George Sheehan, in *Running and Being* (Warner Books, 1978), gives a good description of what takes place in his mind while he exercises.

There is all the while a stream of consciousness, a torrent of ideas, coursing through my brain. One idea after another goes hurtling past like so much white water.

— Dr. George Sheehan

That is the way I feel when I take a brisk walk. My body is more efficient at supplying my brain with nutrients and oxygenated blood when physical exertion is involved. I get my heart pumping, and I breathe better. I often find myself at the end of my walk without noticing the passage of forty-five minutes. Instead of being worn out when I return, I am revitalized, and my thinking is clarified. Regular exercise really and truly improves my quality of life. Exercise releases endorphins, which are natural opiates. And we don't have to bench press Volkswagens to improve our overall health. A vigorous walk will do.

Our bodies are on loan from God, and so it would be blasphemous not to take care of them. We respect this physical housing for our soul by keeping in shape. Regular, conscientious exercise provides us with the dividends of stamina and endurance necessary for the everyday struggles of life.

Just as our muscles will deteriorate when not used, our minds will atrophy if not regularly exercised. They are vulnerable to an inadequate diet, lack of sleep, and lack of exercise. They are also vulnerable to lack of challenge. Rather than allowing ourselves to stagnate in a brain-numbed existence, we can develop an insatiable desire to learn. Our brain is designed to expand its power to meet the demands we place on it. When an activity becomes automatic, it's time to find another mind-stimulating project. Reading is an excellent mental activity. Reading grants us access to a multitude of varied worlds beyond our own. Writing exercises the visualizing, imagining powers we all possess and also exercises our creativity.

In my gerontology coursework, I learned that one of the best investments we can make toward growing older is in friendships. We must make it a priority to invest in relationships, and the appreciation of others. We must stay socially active in order to continually accumulate and foster new relationships, since we will lose more friends through death during our third age than during any other period in our lives. As we age, many of us will lose friends due to illness or death, or we'll somehow lose track of them. These people need to be replaced, or we will end up alone.

Plainly, life is much more enjoyable when shared with other people. Positive connections are a great resource for personal support. Not only will our friendships benefit us, but our families won't have to worry about our welfare as much. Later on, our personal relationships will spare us negative feelings of loneliness, rejection, and isolation.

When my dad was in his sixties, he was reintroduced to a lady friend at one of his high school reunions, and they remained companions until he passed on. While they were together, my brothers, sister and I never had to worry about Dad. While I was thousands of miles away taking care of my own family, it was comforting to know that he and Florence were together. The time spent with her on the weekends gave Dad something to look forward to, got him back into exercise, and he picked up a new interest—the stock market.

It is inevitable that our friendships will evolve over time. Changing dynamics keeps things interesting. Change helps keep us young, and staying active socially helps foster resilience. We must never let a little dispute injure a great friendship.

A lot of my friends play bridge. It is their passion. The possibility of competing into our advanced years is something to be cherished. It's a gift. It also helps mental acuity. I can't imagine playing cards ever being my passion, but on the other hand, my friends probably think I'm nuts pounding away at my keyboard day in and day out.

One of the blessings of living in God's beautiful world is that there is always something new to learn. There are plenty of interests other than just our families and work. We can keep up with current affairs, and stay active with at least one hobby. The rules of the world are constantly changing, and we must remain on top of these. By taking an interest in the world around us, we will be able to change or adapt when necessary.

Since we are always changing, understanding ourselves is an ongoing process. We must continue to maintain our self-awareness, so that we can adjust our goals and behaviors. In order to know our purpose, we must reevaluate our strengths. Self-knowledge is critical. We must recognize the skills we will need for future success, and prepare contingency plans in case of skill loss due to injury or some other unforeseen event (see the chapter '*How am I doing as a Human Being?*').

When discussing flexibility and adaptability, I like the example of the tire meeting the road. When tires were first invented, manufacturers tried to make a tire that would resist the bumps in the road. They were rigid, and couldn't conform to varied conditions. These tires didn't last very long. They weren't flexible, and they couldn't adapt to changing conditions. Then the factories reinvented tires to absorb the unevenness of the road. This type of tire 'took it,' and adjusted to the impact with very little damage. And guess what? These new tires had a much longer life.

We can use this same principle in our lives. We will travel better if we maintain a receptive and flexible perspective. With practice, we'll become more proficient at 'meeting the road' and moving on.

Satisfied Yet Ever Dissatisfied

Some people never seem to grow old. Always active in thought, always ready to adapt new ideas, they are never chargeable to fogeyism. Satisfied yet ever dissatisfied, settled, yet ever unsettled, they always enjoy the best of what is, and are the first to find the best of what will be.

— William Shakespeare

Unstoppable people continually discover new things about themselves and their universe. They continue to grow. Many of us, after we leave the discipline of formal education, let our minds atrophy. We don't think analytically and we don't write, at least not in ways that challenge our ability to express ourselves in clear and concise language.

But formal education is only one way to learn. When we leave school, it takes individual initiative, but by continually making a concerted effort to learn, we make an investment in ourselves on a daily basis. The enemy of mental acuity isn't growing old, but passivity.

Studies suggest the commonsense idea that stimulating the brain with continuous intellectual activity keeps neurons healthy and alive. Our nervous systems continue to grow when they are presented with regular challenges. Education may help the brain's nerve cells to build up more networks, giving it a larger base or reserve from which to draw upon when the neural linkages begin to fade.

Continuing mental activity may also spare us mental confusion down the road that prevents many older people from enjoying life. Not only can our memories be strengthened but, like any muscle, our brain will wither if not used. Our mental efficiency will diminish if it is not properly exercised. Therefore, continually honing and expanding our mind is vital to our mental renewal. And we can take comfort in knowing that we can't use our minds up, or wear them out.

There's something very attractive about an older person with a young, vibrant mind. The best beautifying technique in the world is an active mind that is always finding something new to learn, think about, or just admire. Studies suggest that people with more education are more independent and competent later in life. Statistically, the more education we get, the less likely we are to develop signs of Alzheimer's. Studies have also found that when brains of 30-year-olds and 55-year-olds are compared, the older brains are better developed.

But aging is a clever process. It's not that it's a strong pull, but it's vigilant, tireless and patient. Whenever we permit our mind or body to slow down, the momentum of aging picks up. When we allow weakness to develop anywhere, age will find it, and use it to its advantage.

While the physical aspect of me has begun its decline, my faith more than compensates for any presumed losses. God has taken on a new and more profound meaning.

The blossom vanishes of itself as the fruit grows. So will your lower self vanish as the Divine grows within you.

— Vivekenanda

Aging nudges our spiritual alarm clock, and forces us to set priorities. Realizing that life is short helps us use our time more wisely, and for eternal good. Because our days are numbered, we want our work to be effective and productive.

Many men and women in their seventies, eighties and nineties have contributed richly to the world. The following is a small sampling of people who accomplished their greatest feats only after they were well into their third age: Cato, a prominent Roman statesman, didn't begin to study Greek and *master* the language until the age of 80. Chaucer, the greatest English poet of the Middle Ages, wrote The Canterbury Tales, one of the masterpieces of all literature, not long before he died at the age of 60. Michelangelo continued to paint and write poetry up until just days before he passed away at the age of 89. Countless others are recorded throughout history whose finest hours didn't materialize until they were well into their third age. When will our finest hour be? I hope to find out by never giving in and never giving up.

Selling the Ford

When we grow older, our bodies wear out. Our limiting clay garments are put aside, no longer needed. They have served us well. They have done a magnificent job, but they were only the vehicle on our journey. Now they are in decline, and it's time to trade them in.

I'm not saying to go run out in front of a car. I don't long to die. I take good care of my body, because I want to experience life on earth for as long as possible. God has intended us to live a full and productive life, and we shouldn't spend our days dreading the end.

After a near-death experience, people who recover to describe what happened never mention anguish or pain, or even despair. In fact, they report quite the opposite. They recall a strange feeling of tranquility and peace. I had heard about these events before, but I needed to hear it from someone I trusted, someone who had nothing to gain by telling their story. This corroborating evidence came from a close personal friend of mine.

Elizabeth Klungness, writing coach, mentor, and a good friend of mine, was brought up as a Christian, but admits to not being very spiritual. She gave me permission to include her near-death experience here. It reconfirmed her belief in everlasting life. The following is her story.

"Most people facing major surgery are usually anxious, but what is it we fear? Is it the discomfort, the pain, the indignities, the long nights, the endless poking and prodding by hospital staff? Or is it fear of death?

I think back upon various surgeries I've had in the past—I am one of those who seems to have far too many ailments that require going under the surgeon's knife. One post-op experience I had many years ago changed my life, and made me aware of how fragile my beliefs were, at the same time reinforcing what I had learned as a child in many Sunday School lessons.

There is a hereafter. I am so sure of it that now, as I face yet one more surgery, I find a sense of peace, not apprehension.

My body had performed as expected following abdominal surgery, and I had gone home after a week. Unfortunately, I felt worse and worse as each day went by, and had to return to the hospital six days later, which was a Sunday. It was a military hospital, with two patients to a cubicle. My roommate had a broken leg, which was suspended in the air, leaving her unable to get out of bed.

At that time, we were at the mercy of the nurses, who offered bed pans once, at 10 p.m., whether they were needed or not. I soon trained myself to use them as dictated, because I would not have another opportunity until the next shift came on board at 2 a.m. in the morning. Once the bedpan ritual was over, the nurses retreated to have coffee.

After a half hour, I began to realize that my sheets were wet. My roommate heard a dripping sound, and switched on the light. What she saw was a trickle of blood on the floor between our beds, and so she hit the emergency button.

Finally, a nurse came to see why we weren't being good patients and keeping quiet. One look, and she set the wheels in motion. More surgery and nine pints of blood later, I was back on the ward, but still unconscious. I remained that way for three days.

My only memories of what was happening around me from the time I was wheeled into surgery were of a nurse saying, "She won't be here when I come back in the morning," and the surgeon's question, "What went wrong?"

I didn't rise above my body on the operating table. I didn't enjoy any of the out-of-body experiences I have since read about. What did happen was an overwhelming sense of peace, of moving down something narrow that was brilliantly lit, of someone at the end of the 'tunnel,' as it is usually described. I reached out my arms to embrace this figure, but he or she, I cannot tell you which, kept his or her arms down by their side, and did not move. In my mind, I heard the words, "You must go back."

I didn't want to. It was so peaceful, and the color blue seemed to surround me, almost in waves. I think I just stood there, or floated there, for some time, not speaking, nor hearing anything, just experiencing this complete wrap-around feeling of complete calm. I no longer felt pain, nor harbored worries. I was cuddled, loved, and understood everything.

The next thing I experienced was the feeling of fighting to come to the surface. It was the same feeling you have when you dive into the water and strive to bring your body back up to breathe. It wasn't a struggle, just the feeling of rising from one place to another.

I don't know why I was sent back, what great things I was supposed to accomplish in this world. I only know that if I keep striving to help my fellow man, perhaps to help dispel the fears that many have of death, I will be allowed to stay next time in this glorious peace we call the hereafter."

Near-death experiences are not caused by a lack of oxygen to the brain, or drugs, or psychological stresses evoked by the fear of dying. Almost twenty years of scientific research has documented that these experiences are a natural and normal process...Near-death experiences are absolutely real and not hallucinations of the mind. They are as real as any other human capability.

— Betty J. Eadie *(Embraced by the Light)*

Betty Eadie describes her own near-death experience as "a profoundly pleasant sense of well being and calmness…I had never felt greater tranquility in my life. I was amazed at my ability to comprehend the mysteries of the universe simply by reflecting on them." Betty shows that near-death experiences don't instill a desire to die, but provide us with a desire to live life to the fullest.

It has only been in the last few hundred years that our culture in general has developed the faulty notion that there is no soul in man, and therefore no life everlasting.

Why? I don't know, but the effect has created an unnatural fear of dying that permeates society. Many of our modern problems, from the erosion of family to drug abuse, come from our collective lack of spiritual vision.

Here are a few of my own thoughts on dying. Did you ever notice that after a really horrible life event, something really good happens? There is always a blessing. I've noticed this my entire life. Triumph always follows tragedy. These ups and downs of life continue, even until our passing turns to our last triumph.

They start even before we are born. We were alive in the womb. Wasn't that a wonderful way to live? All of our needs and wants were provided with unconditional love. It was a perfect experience (existence). When we're pushed out into a cold world, we scream because we're afraid. We've never experienced anything like this. Where is the warmth and nourishment we were accustomed to? Now we're forced to cry to let our needs be known. With life come struggles and challenges. Living in the womb was easy, but life was difficult.

Dying can be the hardest part of living. It can be the most physically painful experience for the person at the end of their life, and one of the most emotionally painful experiences for those closest to them.

So, we must ask ourselves what follows. What usually follows tragedy? How about beautiful liberation, or perfect bliss, absolute peace, relief, and deliverance? Total release without suffering? If birth into a difficult world follows the perfect bliss of the womb, shouldn't perfect joy follow the dying process?

Recovery from near death is the ultimate recovery. Those who have had near-death experiences are almost always positively impacted by them. They return with a newfound appreciation and gratitude for the world around them. They have renewed purposes. Some go as far as to say that illness is one of the great privileges of life. Sickness pares and lops off our expendables, leaving us with life's essence.

It turns out that the whole journey of aging is something that is designed to lead us from thinking of ourselves, and we're given opportunity after opportunity to practice letting go. When our bodies start to fail us we can easily become discouraged, unless we remain open-minded. Accepting and benefiting from our soul's vantage point leaves an infinite number of experiences to look forward to and cherish.

As I enter my bonus age, I am more powerful than any rejection, failure or loss that I encounter. I have strength and survivorship, and have triumphed over all kinds of vicissitudes, disappointments, trials and illnesses. This enables me to move forward with confidence, knowing that few of life's storms are devastating enough to knock me out. Even though I will be required to close many more chapters on my journey through life, I am finding that happiness comes much easier, with fewer doubts, fears and needs.

Twelve-step Program Gifts

On June 10, 1935, a phone call from a stockbroker named Bill Wilson to a surgeon named Dr. Bob Smith heralded the birth of Alcoholics Anonymous. Their idea was that two or more alcoholics could abstain from alcohol together more easily than a single alcoholic could alone. The two met that evening in Akron, Ohio, and that same month, a group of alcoholics started the first A.A. meeting.

In 1939, the spiritual 12-step program of recovery was formulated, and the premier edition of the book of Alcoholics Anonymous was printed. Then, in March of 1941, Jack Anderson wrote a feature article in the Saturday Evening Post about Alcoholics Anonymous which caused a deluge of new members. That fellowship has helped thousands get and stay sober, and the flood of participants continues to this day.

The 12-step Recovery Program of A.A. is a simple program, with two main components: the 12 steps themselves, and then the 12-step meetings which support and promote the steps. These 12 steps are based on four ideas: making peace with ourselves; making peace with others; keeping the peace; and spreading the word. Now, doesn't this sound like a fantastic cause?

Well, it may be a wonderful cause, but as you can imagine, when I was first exposed to A.A., sweeping social concepts and great spiritual truths did not immediately come to mind. Becoming an alcoholic was like a death to me. What could be more deplorable than being a drunk! An ALCOHOLIC! And then, to add fat to the fire, I was sentenced to a lifetime of A.A. meetings. To me, these had as much allure as a colonoscopy!

When my treatment center counselors (of which there were many) sent me home, they thought their discharge plan would give me the best opportunity for long-term sobriety. It was a plan that had been studied and perfected over many years, and was widely adopted for its high success rate. The treatment plan that works best for most alcoholics includes strict attendance at and participation in A.A. meetings. However, this well thought out plan worked in reverse for me. It actually drove me back to drinking! What my counselors didn't know was that I suffered from social anxiety. When I thought about talking in front of a group of people, all I wanted to do was drink!

My counselors didn't know about my incapacitating fear because I wasn't screened for it, even though it's commonly known that there is a direct link between alcoholism and social anxiety disorder. A few simple questions upon admittance to determine co-existing illnesses that might undermine a person's recovery would be my suggestion to substance abuse treatment professionals. Diagnosis of my underlying conditions could have meant a modified treatment strategy. It also would have saved my family and me years and years of anguish.

Not knowing about these other illnesses, my counselors went ahead and ordered me into situations that I used to turn to drink over, immediately sabotaging my recovery! I suffered endlessly and needlessly, because I was initially treated only for my alcoholism, and not for the causes of my substance abuse. For years, sitting in A.A. meetings was sheer agony for me. I never heard any of the comforting or encouraging words (the important stuff), because all my mind could do was relentlessly rehearse what I would say if called upon.

I remember my first few meetings. All I could do was cry. How could a nice girl like me end up in a place like this? I was filled with shame, guilt, remorse, and anger at this disgraceful turn of events.

My big concern at the time was that I had a life to lead, and these meetings were disruptions in my day! As if the Earth would go into a holding pattern without my drunken input. To me, meetings were inane, useless, and a total waste of time. With my mind in such turmoil, I couldn't relate to any of the people, and I couldn't attempt to get to know them either, which is one of the main reasons for attending meetings in the first place!

I couldn't understand these A.A. people, with all their enthusiasm, nor could I understand their happiness. They were laughing, and having fun, and they kept calling themselves grateful alcoholics. What the heck? I was sitting with not only a bunch of drunks, but a bunch of liars as well. There was a pain inside me that only alcohol could crush. Who were they to tell me to give it up, and live with the pain?

Then, as if reading my mind, some little old lady would pat my knee, and gently tell me that things would get better if I just kept coming back. This threw me into immediately wondering what effect my knitting needle might have on her maddening cheerfulness. Continuing with my mind's rant, I quickly dismissed ever coming back.

How could they be grateful alcoholics? It was November, and the holidays were looming. What would Christmas be like without festive eggnog, or New Year's Eve without champagne? Their gratitude was grating on my last few available nerves, leaving me *quite* testy, and very, very angry. My main goal in life was to get people to think highly of me. I wanted prestige! Sitting in A.A. meetings didn't quite jive with that concept.

How could anyone in their right mind want to be here? I kept thinking, "You're all 'Looney Tunes.'" But once again, I was pleasantly reminded that when we jump out of an airplane, it is highly recommended that we pull our ripcord. And then they related this to the recovery process. To remain sober, it was highly recommended that I become an active member of Alcoholic's Anonymous.

Another problem I had with these people was all the God talk. They were a bunch of drunks, so how could they be spouting off about God? They not only wanted me to stop drinking, but they also wanted me to start telling everybody how much I loved God. Well, God hadn't been so kind to me lately, and I wasn't so sure I liked Him anymore. Again, after hearing me out, they politely told me that I needed to find a God I could do business with. They said this with reverence, which immediately sent me looking for my knitting needle again.

To add to my pile of grievances, the program clichés didn't seem to address my drinking problem. Actually, it wasn't a drinking problem. I was good at drinking. It was a stopping problem. What did *first things first* have to do with me staying sober?

Nonetheless, I was sick and tired of being sick and tired. I was finally defeated enough to at least listen to what these people had to say, and something I said or read kept bringing me back. After all, they were happy, and I wasn't. Besides that, I had nowhere else to go. I wasn't exactly frolicking in the sunshine of public adulation, and I felt like the dregs of humanity. So, I sat for a while listening to 'keep it simple,' or 'KISS—keep it simple stupid,' 'let go and let God' and 'one day at a time.'

Only after I had been effectively treated for social anxiety did A.A. work for me, and then it worked beautifully. It took a long time to accept my situation, and realize that the members of Alcoholics Anonymous share a special bond that is deeper than mere camaraderie. There was a spiritual connectedness that only those who have stood at death's door, and been spared, could understand. I was beginning to realize that these people weren't a bunch of brain-dead, flipped out, crazy head cases after all. They were not losers, but very much a bunch of winners. Finally, although it would take a while, I too would become a gusher of gratitude.

The Light From Many Lamps

Meetings are a gold mine of life experiences, the mother lode of what to do and what not to do. A.A. meetings follow the 12-step program of recovery, guiding us toward a better life. But for me, the shelf life of these ideas is about 24 hours. I have to be reminded all the time.

With the disease of alcoholism, sick minds need to heal along with sick bodies. It was in A.A. where I learned honesty, forgiveness and gratitude. In A.A., I learned to live life on life's terms, and it was there that I was brought back to God.

There is nothing like the collective wisdom of a group of people, particularly a group who have been set back, and are now moving forward with grace and dignity. I don't have to make every mistake in the world—someone else has done that, and will share about it. My fellow recoverees talk about their mistakes, and when they do, it helps me keep from making the same ones. Sitting before me are my life coaches, and some of my best friends. There is more I need to learn, and meetings provide me access to the vast resource and potential of other human beings.

I can only explain how spiritually powerful the program of Alcoholics Anonymous is by relating a true story told by Chuck C. in *A New Pair of Glasses*. Chuck tells us about a Jesuit priest, Father Ed Dowling, who was not an alcoholic, but worked with a lot of us. He was around at the beginning of Alcoholics Anonymous back in 1935.

Father Ed said that he never had a problem with alcohol, but his problem was lack of faith. Imagine a priest without faith! I'm sure Chuck C. was just as astonished as I was when he heard this. Father Ed confessed that he had gone through eighteen years of school, completed all of his seminary studies, and was even ordained, but hadn't *really* believed. He said he finally came to believe in God by watching what happened to us in Alcoholics Anonymous. A priest came to believe by watching the miracles in A.A.!

Miracles took place back in 1935, and they are still happening today. I see them all the time.

Why I Still go to Meetings

Years ago, our fathers' and forefathers' attitudes were shaped during childhood by observing how other family members reacted to adversity. Families were their social support systems. But families for a large part aren't around anymore. Both parents work, grandparents live far away, and TVs and computers are used as surrogates. Gone are the comforting rituals of family life. These conditions have created a great need for support groups, places to go where we can download our troubles without criticism.

The high divorce rate has caused further disintegration of the family, and even in households where there is still a family, many homes don't provide a spiritual foundation. For some people, 12-step meetings provide the only pathway to God.

After more than 13 years in recovery, people ask me why I *still* go to meetings. There are many reasons why I remain a regular. Today, I know that for me, alcohol is a thief in the night that is capable of stealing my life. So, the number one reason I continue to attend meetings is that I'm an alcoholic. My disease is an 'ism,' not a 'wasm.' For the rest of my life, I will remain at high risk of sliding back down the slippery slope of alcoholism, and chances are, if I 'went out' (program talk for getting drunk), I wouldn't make it back to sobriety. Last time I 'went out,' it was nuclear war, and I came within inches of death. Another reason I remain an active member of A.A. is that a key ingredient for solid sobriety is to remain connected with others in recovery. It's been shown time and time again that alcoholics who drop out of the program invariably relapse into substance abuse and old destructive behaviors. God gave me this program as a tool, so I need to use it.

Since the quality of my life is affected by the people I associate with, I want to associate with people who make good choices. Today, I enjoy hanging out with people who are taking a good hard look at themselves on a daily basis.

The beauty of the A.A. program is that spirituality is expressed in universal terms. There is a spiritual inclusiveness. A.A. meetings allow people from every religion to join in and share our spiritual nourishment. We accept God, pray, and enjoy fellowship with each other, but we leave the theology to each individual's own beliefs. It is a way of life that conflicts with no-ones religion or beliefs, and A.A. has the unqualified support of nearly every religious organization.

Right before me in every meeting are people whose lives have been transformed. From Park Avenue to the park bench, we drunks don't suffer from a shortage of experience. From painters and truck drivers to doctors and P.T.A. presidents, I need to hear the message repeated over and over again. My frame of mind determines who I will relate to best at the time.

I need to be reminded often about my wretched past, and how I can continue the betterment of me. When I meet newcomers, I am able to recall the agony of my sickness. I remember how awful I felt, and then I am grateful for how far I've come. Meetings keep the grass green, and give me a release from my 'uniqueness.' I am given comfort just knowing that I am not alone.

I think about the 13- and 14-year-olds in recovery today. These kids are being turned around from a possible life of crime and imprisonment to a spiritual life committed to God's purpose. I know my goal at age 13 certainly wasn't spiritual progress. My goal was to have fun, and hang out with my friends. Today, the young people in recovery from substance abuse still have these same goals, but they have God hanging out with them, too. They seek His direction, and their lives are under His care. They are having 'the time of their lives.' I see the pride in their faces. The meaning and significance of their lives will make an incredible impact for many generations to come.

Drinking was my life, my comfort, my God. I need people to teach me on an ongoing basis how to live a good life without it. Today, I *still* love my A.A. meetings. I love watching people get better. I love seeing people turn their lives around. When a resource such as meetings is available to me, I enjoy taking advantage of it in my quest to be all I can and ought to be.

Meetings remind me to use all of the tools in my twelve-step survival tool kit. One of the tools is the serenity prayer, which is recited at every meeting for good reasons.

God grant me the serenity to accept the things I cannot change, courage to change the things I can, and wisdom to know the difference.

When we come upon a potential train wreck in our lives, we can stop and ask ourselves, "Can I change this situation?" Answering "yes" or "no" and moving forward accordingly can save us a lot of aggravation. The serenity prayer helps me break down and analyze situations that used to baffle me. Simply by doing this, I make the situation more manageable.

A big portion of the serenity prayer is about acceptance. On page 449 (page has changed in newer editions) of *The Big Book of Alcoholics Anonymous* there is another tool that is well known to regular meeting attendees. The following paragraph contains the key points of the message:

And acceptance is the answer to all my problems today. When I am disturbed, it is because I find some person, place, thing, or situation—some fact of my life—unacceptable to me, and I can find no serenity until I accept that person, place, thing or situation as being exactly the way it's supposed to be at this moment. Nothing, absolutely nothing happens in God's world by mistake. Until I could accept my alcoholism, I could not stay sober; unless I accept life completely on life's terms, I cannot be happy. I need to concentrate not so much on what needs to be changed in the world as on what needs to be changed in me and in my attitudes.

So often I find myself applying this paragraph to the problem before me, or the problem my mind has created.

In meetings, we experience unconditional love, a love some of us have never known. In meetings, I see multifaceted joy. While an unthinking world may look upon the people who attend A.A. meetings as a bunch of slobs and reprobates, we who are in attendance feel a triumph of spirit, a triumph of humility over false pride and self-centeredness. Those of us in recovery share the release from the bondage of self, and from enslavement we are set free. Meetings have worked so well for recovering alcoholics that there are now support groups for cancer survivors, diabetics and sufferers of many other conditions. Many of these programs are modeled after A.A.

Finally, I go to 12-step meetings because I continually hear inspiring stories, like the following one from Kathy B., which I am retelling here to the best of my ability, with her permission. The subject of the meeting was the difference between a 'spiritual awakening' and 'spiritual awareness.' In her story, you'll see Kathy's awakening, and her renewed inner connectedness with people.

Kathy B.'s Story

"It was 1967, the summer of love, and the Beatles were the rage. I was seventeen, and nine months pregnant. An overcast day in Dayton, Ohio contributed to the stifling humidity, and my ankles were swollen enough to compete with my stomach for attention. After a series of contractions alerted me that it was time, my mom and I sat side by side on the long journey to the hospital. During the final few weeks of my pregnancy, many heart-wrenching conversations about motherhood had consumed our time but now, an anxious silence prevailed. Again, we were thrown back together by default, compensating for my dad's distance and my boyfriend's abandonment. Long ago, my dad's love for booze had left little room for my mother or me.

The previous September, my boyfriend and I had found ourselves with runaway desires. Youthful indiscretions soon followed. The idea of a baby unnerved my boyfriend, and he soon left me. I do not fault him for his decision; we were both still kids. Hard choices would come to hound me most of my life; having a child at age seventeen would be far from my most difficult one.

Sitting in the car, I felt my eyes flood with tears. The pain welled up, spilled over, and wet my neck. Sadness came and swallowed me. Desperate and fearful, I hunched deeper into myself and trembled like a wounded, overweight bird.

Months ago, my high school friends had disappeared. Each sighted puny reasons for deserting me. 'We have nothing in common.' 'She doesn't want to do anything; she's always tired.' 'She's not fun to be around anymore.' Hating my friends and their freedom, I suffered through the remainder of my junior year of high school. Everyone had begun to talk about going away to college, but I knew experiences such as dormitories and sororities would never be mine.

Some girls my age who were 'in the family way' left town when they 'began to show.' Vacationing was not an option for me, since my parents had no money to send me away. Besides, I didn't want to be alone. I wanted to finish the school year, and went back to class, but I felt miserable every day. Finally, the last day arrived, but the ensuing summer days offered little relief. Each seemingly endless twenty-four hours dissolved into the next.

Now, desperate for any diversion on our way to the hospital, I flipped on the car radio. One of the ever-popular Beatles songs was playing.

When I find myself in times of trouble, Mother Mary comes to me, speaking words of wisdom, let it be, let it be. And in my hour of darkness, she is standing right in front of me, speaking words of wisdom, let it be, let it be.

At that point, I felt a calm presence envelope the car, and a quiet sense of empowerment overtook me. I realized that God was speaking to me, that I didn't have to do this alone. The words and melody comforted me during the long birthing process, when sadness sabotaged any hope for joy, but this fleeting faith that swept through me during my time of need then receded, to lay dormant and not surface again until years later.

With less than total enthusiasm, I delivered my little Allison into the world. A giant heartache was our only companion. With no idea of how I would take care of my baby girl, I isolated myself in self-pity. My life limped along, and I turned from dreaming to surviving. I felt like my life's ambitions had been reduced to the company of a crying child. The lanes of my life narrowed, and single motherhood exacted its toll. Via various controlled substances, I sought mind-numbing relief. I figured that if I didn't feel, I couldn't hurt.

My life continued to deteriorate, and I developed a chemical dependency so deep-rooted it nearly cost me everything. With a new baby, and no self-esteem, I latched onto the first man who seemed interested. From the beginning, our relationship was disastrous. Our only common interests were drugs and alcohol, which threatened to destroy us both. Our short marriage was a difficult one and, not happy with it or what I had become, I sought help. Having seen my father deteriorate into alcoholism made me want something better. I admitted myself into an outpatient program, and managed to stop using and abusing drugs and alcohol, but my husband could not.

I waited a few years for him to surface from his addictions, but he never did. When even prayers didn't help, I finally gave him an ultimatum. He needed to stop drinking, or I would take Allison and leave. I was finally feeling too good about myself to have my life ruined again. Realizing that I could make a better life for my little girl, I took Allison and left.

By working at a local restaurant, I managed to get through nursing school. I taught Allison about God, and how He was always with us in one form or another. I was happy to teach her about God, and she thrived right along with me. I made close friends with other people who were regaining control of their lives, and slowly my life turned around.

It took me a number of years in recovery before I considered any formal religion, but one day a friend of mine asked if I was ready to try church again. I hadn't attended in years, but I agreed to go along, and took my now thirty-two-year-old daughter Allison and her new baby girl along, too.

When the four of us entered the chapel, I expected to hear *Amazing Grace* or some other regular church hymn but instead, what I heard was:

And when the night is cloudy, there is still a light that shines on me, shine until tomorrow, let it be, let it be. I wake up to the sound of music, Mother Mary comes to me, speaking words of wisdom, let it be, let it be.

Sweet sounds painted the air with hope, as I listened to those beautiful words once again. God's amazing power had turned the work of an English rock group into music from Him. This same melody bought me back to the day I sat, pregnant, riding to the hospital with my mom, and I was filled with an overwhelming peace. I had come home."

Today, Kathy is striving to be the best person she can be. I see the progress she has made, and her story reminds me that anything is possible with God by my side. It also helps me immensely to know that I am not alone in my disease, and that many people's 'bottoms' are a lot lower that mine.

The Humble Don't Stumble

Humility is often misunderstood. I found a good definition of it on page 58 of *The Twelve Steps and Twelve Traditions*. This book, put out by Alcoholics Anonymous, explains in detail the spiritual process of the 12 steps. Humility is described as 'a clear recognition of what and who we are, followed by a sincere attempt to become what we could be.' Humility is an integral part of the 12-step process. To me, it is wearing the cloak of humanness with grace and dignity.

The desire to work toward humility as a beneficial goal in and of itself has taken me a long time to accept, but today, the notion that I could run my life by myself, and call on Him only when needed, has evaporated. Today, I humble myself before Him on a daily basis.

Our ego, an essential tool for everyday living, and necessary for our existence, oftentimes exceeds its proper function. Our instincts to possess material and emotional security, or merely to feel important, will oftentimes lead us way off course. Unless they are held in check, our egos can lead us into trouble.

Humility requires many of us to reverse our natural desires. When we keep our appetites in check, we are better able to accept God's will for us, and become channels for His purpose. The more we have God in our lives, the better our egos keep to their useful purposes, but I still battle with my ego every day. It still needs to be subdued, controlled and mastered.

One way to keep our egos reined in is to be in constant realization that we are not the power behind our successes. Just because my will has finally come into alignment with God's doesn't mean that I can take the credit for my progress.

Humility clears the mind, and makes unclouded vision possible. It keeps us from trampling on others. All I have to do is attend an A.A. meeting to remember from whence I came, and for humility to kick back in. At every meeting, we openly proclaim our biggest character defect, describing ourselves truthfully for everyone to hear: "I'm Vivian, and I'm an alcoholic." At the meetings I attend, there are almost always newcomers, and I see the shame, guilt, pain, and fear well up and pour out from their sick and very tired eyes.

Turning our will over to the care of God is one of the basic ingredients of humility. And when we humble ourselves before Him, our failure and suffering become priceless assets. Today, I don't have to outperform or outmaneuver everyone else. It is not me against the world anymore. I was fighting a battle that didn't need to be fought. As a matter of fact, I now go around building everybody else up!

We Can Only Keep it if We Give it Away

For the longest time, I didn't quite understand this statement. Just like science and religion, the 12-step program of recovery has many paradoxes. The concept that 'we have to give it away to keep it' has to do with step twelve:

Having had a spiritual awakening as the result of these Steps, we tried to carry this message to others, and to practice these principles in all our affairs.

I started helping others because that's what step number twelve said to do. Today, I comprehend the fact that when I help people, I make myself stronger in the process. Every time I help another alcoholic, I am strengthening my own sobriety.

When I talk to those who are newly sober, I'm reminded of how afraid I was, and I keep these awful memories green.

As a group, we keep our umbrellas open, and carry them over one another. We support and comfort one another. When I nurture fellow members along their spiritual journey, I'm encouraged in my faith, and by keeping my friendships in A.A., I am strengthened and encouraged in my recovery.

Happy Roads of Recovery

If I stopped going to meetings, I would miss all my friends. Because we only use our first names in meetings, we sometimes have to differentiate if we have a number of Bobs, Kathys, or other common names. So, at my 7 a.m. meeting in town, I would miss golfing Bob, lawyer Bob, big Bob, and crazy Bob (he's the first to admit that he is one sandwich short of a picnic, and he says this with a joyful heart). And then I'd miss tiny Kathy, pill head Kathy (she calls herself this), and real estate Kathy. I'd miss them all, and how they were doing on their respective happy roads of destiny.

The 12-step program, when fleshed out, really comes down to love and service, and its wisdom focuses on how to live happily according to God's plan. This program offers a prescription for living from which anyone can benefit. Like many others, I needed a simple numbered plan, for I was sick, sad and sorry as only the dying could be.

Today, my struggles have given me the opportunity to help others. It is my experience as an alcoholic that makes me of unique value to the person who still suffers. Being free of fear enables me to free someone else, and being able to do well while helping others is one of the greatest joys in my life today.

No matter what is happening in my life, or what feelings are troubling me, the program offers a foundation for the attainment of inner peace. God is my guide, protector and loving Father, while A.A. provides a numbered 12-step path to facilitate my journey. I'm on the comeback ladder, and I like where I'm headed. I don't want to mess with that, and I don't want to miss out on anything God sends my way.

The Most Powerful Force in the Universe

There is a deep void within all of us, and this yearning for completeness or fulfillment is where the fundamental idea of God lies. Faith in a power greater than ourselves and its miraculous demonstration in our lives is as old as man himself. The divine spark is in each of us, and we have three choices regarding this. We can disregard it, we can turn away, or we can move closer to Him.

We all know in our heart of hearts, through our most profound thoughts and experiences, that there is more to living than what we see, hear, smell and touch. Deep down, we know and believe. At times, our faith may be obscured by calamity, pomp, ego, or by worship of other things, but in some form or another, it is there. Many people make vain attempts to fill this emptiness with worldly stuff. During my lifetime, I've substituted God with many different things in an effort to fill that nagging void, none of which provide His great and everlasting love. Only He can successfully fill this vacuum.

People with a belief system seem to enjoy a much greater measure of happiness than other people I have had the pleasure to meet. We seem to wrestle more effectively with life, because we know that we are not alone on our journey. That, right there, should be reason enough to reconnect with God. With Him, my closeness to others deepens. My relationships are richer and more rewarding. He is my ally who smoothes out the peaks and valleys, and makes my journey's crooked paths worthwhile.

Without Him, I'd be a slave to my wants and desires. Without Him, I'd be a plant without light. How can I not depend on a creative power that is absolutely unlimited and bigger than any problem I will ever encounter? I know today that without Him, I could never quite live up to my full potential, nor be as happy as I am on a daily basis.

Remember how important habits are? Well, what drives habits? Our beliefs! His way is the direct path to the development of good habits. A friend put it to me this way. What have we got to lose by believing in Him? If nothing else, believe as a precaution. Pascal looked at believing in God very logically. He suggested that we place our bet that He exists. If He does, we win it all. If He doesn't, we don't lose a thing, but have gained a joyous way to live. Believe without hesitation, because if nothing else, it's the smart thing to do.

With God, the Good News Always Trumps the Bad

God is a fertile human resource that many of us never think to utilize unless we were brought up to do so. And even then, many of us decide, somewhere along the way, that maybe we don't really need God. We begin to feel that we're doing right fine without Him, thank you very much.

But faith in a higher power, who I choose to call God, is the only way to solve many of the mysteries of life. The real questions (Where did I come from? What am I doing here? Where do I go when I die?) cannot be answered scientifically and philosophically. Science might provide good guesses, but there have never been concrete answers. With too many questions unanswered, unless we believe in something, we are without a foundation and without direction. No matter how much I comprehend, there will always be something beyond my understanding. God is the most coherent interpretation of everything I experience. He has answered questions that once plagued me, and my confidence in Him continues to grow on a daily basis.

How can we have values without anything to base them on? By believing in Him and living a Godly life, I automatically save myself many problems. He provides simplification and clarification. I never have to worry about my life anymore, because it is in His hands. What a freedom. With God by my side, no matter how bad things seem to be, everything is still okay.

Strengthening our relationship with God keeps us connected with our innermost values and principles so that our goals will continually reflect His will. If we've gone off-course, we can redo our maps to stay in harmony with our personal source of strength.

Using Him not only as a foundation but also as a *catalyst* for the source of doing good gives me a multitude of advantages. With God, I have a rich feeling of continuous harmony with a universal constructive force.

The government of the United States was set in the context of belief in a higher or divine law. God is in our pledge, in our national anthem, in nearly every patriotic song, and in our founding documents. *In God We Trust* is our national motto, printed on our currency, and we turn to Him in prayer in times of crisis. All our fathers, grandfathers and other people who have come before us could not have been wrong.

He Illuminates the Road Before Me

With God by my side, I can face any loss that comes my way, knowing that I still have Him. Almost every day I want to shout "Hallelujah!" When I'm living by God's will, I have an untroubled heart, because I know I'm doing the right thing. Without Him, I would suffer a terrible sense of isolation. Without God as a resource to handle even the small problems that regularly appear, I'd be at the whim of the wind. With God, the threat of emptiness and meaninglessness disappears. With God, I feel complete. As my partnership with Him matures, my life improves.

Many of us place God far down on our list of priorities. For a long time, I had Him placed right under tennis and just before golf (I don't even play golf). I couldn't be bothered with spiritual connectedness, nor could I see any benefit in it. I had no desire to be close to God. Sure, I admired the little old ladies who read their

Bible every day and did all these good deeds, but I had places to go, people to meet and 'conditions' to 'medicate.' I was way too hip, slick and cool to bother with God. I pushed God off, saying that maybe when I grew old and had more time, I'd look into what He had to say.

For a long time, I felt the same way about God as my kids felt about me and their dad when they were teenagers. They felt that, basically, we didn't know very much. They didn't realize that we had already been through so much of what they were experiencing, and just might have some of the answers to their perplexing questions. But no, they were invincible, and they weren't going to do things Mom and Pop's way.

At some point in our lives, many of us turn away from the religion that was taught by our parents. Our broader horizons tell us that Mom and Dad's way of living isn't the only way to live. Our friends all get along quite well without Judaism, Christianity or other religions, and at this stage we relate better to our peers than we do to our parents. We begin to think that our parents are *very* narrow-minded. I had been fooled before by thoughts of Santa Claus and other false identities, and I wasn't up to any more of that. I wanted evidence. I wanted proof.

At this same time in our lives, we're also exposed to negatives. Some of this comes in the form of immediate gratification (gangs, drugs, alcohol, cults) that can further detour us. Obscured until we are in trouble and need Him desperately, we finally call out to Him, but by only coming to Him in a crisis, we miss His everyday love and comfort. The sad thing is that many who turn away from Him never make it back, and I often think about everything they miss!

Sometime in our lives (some reach this point sooner than others), we realize that our parents aren't so dumb after all. After a few years of difficult reversal, I realized that maybe, just maybe, my life might run a little better under God's direction. My will didn't seem to be working all that well, anyway.

When I finally sobered up, I had a hard time with everything, and the concept of God was no exception. I kept hearing the *God* word, but I just wasn't ready at first. I didn't need that religious stuff; I just needed to fix my life! I had to work on the physical part of my recovery first, and focus just on not drinking myself into oblivion.

After all, I had been spiritually bankrupt, with no real belief system. Alcohol had become my God. It had cured my depression and social phobia when nothing else worked for me. How could I not love my self-discovered solution to my dual ailments? I had found a true friend—who needed God? He had never 'fixed' things for me.

Accepting GOD as **G**ood **O**rderly **D**irection was a good way to let Him back into my life without a big fuss. This seemed to work okay while I continued to heal. Meanwhile, I had just been doing the next indicated thing and managing to stay sober. Finally, I was beginning to feel a little more comfortable in my own skin for the first time in my life.

Professionals say that with addiction, spirituality is the first to leave and the last to return, and this was certainly true with me. After about a year, I began to develop enough clarity of thought to begin pondering the spiritual aspect of life, but I had to keep in mind that I didn't become an alcoholic overnight, I didn't hit bottom until a long time after that, and I certainly wasn't going to become a spiritual pillar of strength immediately, either.

The Russian roulette I was playing with my life gradually began to lose its allure, and when I finally surrendered to recovery, I began to see that people actually enjoyed having God in their lives. I began to see the blessings of the spirit in the people around me. That was a big revelation for me, and I gradually became open to the idea of faith in a higher power. For about a year, I prayed for Him to come into my life.

I embarked on this compulsory scientific experiment because I was finally willing to accept help. I tested the hypothesis that if I acted as if I had faith, I would start to have faith. Sometimes, when we act as if, we leave a little leeway for God to come in. I now understand that when prayers seem to be going unanswered, it doesn't mean He's not listening. Often, it means that he has something better in store for us.

When I finally started to talk to Him, I didn't feel His ferocious love or anything close to that. He and I didn't connect right away. I wanted to say, like so many do, "He's not answering my prayers. This praying stuff is a bunch of baloney." But the thing is, God's time and mine doesn't always jive when it comes to answering my desperate sniveling. After all, He's got eternity, and all I've got is now.

At first, my attempt to walk the talk was like trudging through peanut butter. I didn't experience any overwhelming warm glow of comfort until much later. There was no 'bright light on the road to Damascus' for me. But just as we can't pull the rose petals open to experience the beautiful bloom, we can't force a loving relationship with Him either. It just happened one day, when I noticed that He was indeed working in my life. He was right beside me in everything I did. I was happier, and more serene. What a gift, never to be alone! It was exactly what I longed for, and desperately needed. And to this day, I'm still surprised that I'm *actually* spiritual— that's how off-course I was.

Some people say religion is just a crutch. It's no more a crutch than our cars that take us to our local grocery store. Motorized travel helps us accomplish our goals more efficiently. God is there to help us and to guide us, too.

If We had all the Answers, There'd be no Room for Faith

Why does He make it difficult for some of us to believe? Now that's a question that used to haunt me all the time. But aren't we all drawn to the mysterious? All-knowingness would cause us to stop seeking, to stop wondering and to stop learning. Absolute certainty would destroy our reason for being. There is a joy to be found in the many mysteries of life, and we'd be denied this if we knew it all.

It's not always easy believing in God, because we can't force Him into a mold we can understand. He is so powerful, so awesome, so all-encompassing, that our teeny-weeny brains can't conceive anything on that scale or of that magnitude. All our ideas are only relative to what we perceive in a universe whose very scale is beyond our grasp.

Because of our confined perspective, we will probably never see the true reality of our situation, and when we realize that our understanding will always be lacking, we open the door for acceptance. We must have faith to a certain degree.

God is around forevermore, but He's just not always packaged the way we'd expect. Let me illustrate this. If we take white sand and then mix it with black sand, we get gray sand. This is very easy to demonstrate and observe. But a microscopic insect moving among the grains of sand will only see giant black and white boulders. On this insect's scale of observation, there is no such thing as gray sand. Its only perceives black and white boulders. Like the insect's view, our view of the world is *extremely* limited. God's view shows not only the bigger picture (gray sand), but also the smaller picture (black and white boulders). So, to keep things very simple…His view is best!

Ever since Darwin advanced his theory of evolution, many people began to look at man as merely a biological accident. Skeptics at the time insisted that science had finally delivered the death blow to faith, but even science is beginning to be tempered by a respect for the incomprehensible mysteries of life and of faith.

Up until the 1950s, no scientist had delved more deeply into the mechanisms of matter than Dr. Robert A. Millikan. He was the first person to determine the charge and mass of the electron, the smallest particle in the universe. Three years before he died, the 82-year-old Nobel Prize-winning scientist, who was head of the California Institute of Technology, in speaking to the country's leading physicists, told them that a lifetime of scientific research had convinced him that there is a divinity that shapes the destiny of man. This same realization has occurred over and over again since the beginning of mankind. I don't have room here to include all the many brilliant minds throughout history that have come to the same conclusion.

As if by infallible instinct, many of the greatest men of all time have turned to God for help. They seem to bypass seductive intellectual doubt, finding a shortcut to universal truth.

I have had so many evidences of His direction, so many instances when I have been controlled by some other power than my own will, that I cannot doubt that this power comes from above. I frequently see my way clear to a decision when I am conscious that I have not sufficient facts upon which to found it.

— Abraham Lincoln

When I returned to the Almighty, I was built up. Being built up, I am bigger than any discouragement, setback or failure. Because of my small brain, I don't know how else to say it. I've heard all kinds of metaphors—'He's in the helicopter, I'm in the traffic jam.' 'God's problem, not mine.' I'm saying those things all the time now.

The spiritual rewards of a relationship with Him include immense dividends in terms of happiness and peace of mind. He is the strength in my life. When I need His wisdom, He's always there.

In A.A. meetings, people talk about their remarkable transformation. Every single one of them explains how they did it, and every single one of them will tell you that they did it by turning their wills and their lives over to the care of God as they understood Him. These are people who were about as far away from God as any of us will ever get.

If the alcoholic or addict can reconnect with God, anybody can.

Knowing that He will never desert me or forsake me is an incredible gift. There is no peace like the profound peace of knowing that God is working in my life. My God is a beautiful, perfect light that guides me through the deep, dark pathways of my journey. All I have to do is believe, in order to enjoy the benefits of His love. It is also an added benefit to the world that this divine companionship powerfully influences our everyday thoughts and actions, creating an atmosphere for compassion and empathy for all of mankind.

His Way is the Highway

Many of us ignore the difficult road of spiritual growth. For those of you who are tottering on the fence, who's the boss of your life? You, with all your human imperfections? Faith requires courage, initiative, independence of thought, and action. Many people don't want God in their lives, because they say He makes things too difficult. What's so hard? I find nothing hard about securing the most powerful force in the universe as my very best friend. He makes things easy for me. Everything I don't want, I give to Him! And He gladly accepts *all* my yucky stuff. To whom else can I turn over all of my problems and have them accepted graciously?

Looking back, I have no idea why it took me so long to find God. He is everywhere and the essence of everything! Searching for God is like trying to find the round part of a basketball. It is the whole thing and everything that it consists of. And just like the basketball which doesn't play very well without its roundness, we don't operate very well without Him. God is all that counts. That's all there is to it.

A guest speaker at our church had just flown over from England and used this as a metaphor, explaining that he hadn't really *flown*. You see, it's impossible for any human being to fly. We can blame this fact on the law of gravity, but there are other many other laws in our universe. Diametrically opposed to the law of gravity is the law of aerodynamics, which cancels the effects of gravity. There is no way he could fly, but he could be flown when he was in union with an airplane. We fly by being flown, by being in union with God. And so, just like flying is impossible without an airplane, many dimensions of living are impossible without God. He makes the impossible possible when I am in union with Him.

I know now what living without Him is like, and what living with Him is all about. With God I have faith, hope and a positive way of life. Without Him, I have none of these things. Without God, life has no meaning; there is only boredom and despair. The rewards of a continual conscious closeness to God far outweigh any effort necessary to remain close to Him. The bottom line is that, no matter how good our life is, with faith…it's better.

Wise Men Still Follow Him

Being a Christian is so deeply rooted in my soul that I cannot imagine believing differently. Given the love Christ so freely demonstrated to me, it was impossible for me not to love Him in return. After listening to the testimony of other Christians and *actually studying* the Bible, I challenge anyone not to soften their heart to Jesus.

I have daily reassurance that believing in Jesus Christ is the right thing to do. I, for one, know from firsthand experience that Christ is much better than any ancient or modern day alternative. But if I had to give an explanation as to why I am a Christian, rather than a Buddhist or a Marxist or a Muslim, I believe in Him for four reasons: to live a better life, to overcome existential angst (anxiety over the why of being, among other things), to better realize my potential, and to embrace hope.

I am a Christian because, after returning to Him, I started to see beautiful changes in the way I handled my life. Today, I have friends who really care about my well-being. I find career-related things working out in ways they never have before, and all the fragmented pieces of my life make much more sense.

I now know that God has, through my faith in Jesus, redeemed my life from that of aimlessness and ungodliness and has made me a new person. I received salvation (eternal life), not based upon my righteous acts, but upon the righteousness of God in Jesus, and I know that nothing can separate me from Him. Where I once was dead on the inside, He has made me alive, alive in Him.

Yes, Jesus gives me purpose and meaning in life, and the ability to fulfill it. His word has given me the power to overcome any difficulty. His joy gives me strength to live joyfully, day by day. I am continually replenished with the 'Fruit of the Spirit,' a biblical term that sums up the nine visible attributes of a true Christian life.

These are: love, joy, peace, longsuffering, gentleness, goodness, faith, meekness and temperance.

When I Say, "I Am A Christian"

When I say, "I am a Christian"
I'm not shouting "I am saved"
I'm whispering "I get lost!"
"That is why I chose this way"

When I say, "I am a Christian"
I don't speak of this with pride.
I'm confessing that I stumble—
Needing God to be my guide

When I say, "I am a Christian"
I'm not trying to be strong.
I'm professing that I'm weak
And pray for strength to carry on

When I say, "I am a Christian"
I'm not bragging of success
I'm admitting that I've failed
And cannot ever pay the debt

When I say, "I am a Christian"
I'm not claiming to be perfect
My flaws are too visible
But God believes I'm worth it

When I say, "I am a Christian"
I still feel the sting of pain
I have my share of heartache
which is why I seek His name

When I say..."I am a Christian"
I do not wish to judge
I have no authority,
I only know I'm loved

More than 2000 years ago, a little boy was born in a stable in the little town of Bethlehem. His first bed was made of straw. He grew up to work as a carpenter and as an adult, never traveled more than 90 miles from His home. He preached about the love of God and one another for only three years, and to only a few thousand people, but during this time He performed many miracles, including healing the sick. Then He was falsely accused and crucified at the age of 33. Finally, according to God's plan, He was resurrected, and ascended back into heaven.

God loved all of us enough to send His only Son, Jesus, into the world that He, being born of the Virgin Mary, might take on the nature of humanity, and live a life of perfect obedience before the Father. God recognized that our greatest need was forgiveness, therefore He sent us His son as our savior so that we could be forgiven our transgressions. Jesus made peace with the Father on my behalf, so that through faith in Him, I might receive His many blessings.

For Those Who Need Proof

Christianity is not a blind faith. The Christian faith is rooted in reality, not in legend or myth. It is the only religion to prove itself. Jesus Christ is the only man who taught the full truth about God and actually demonstrated it.

This extraordinary claim that Jesus is the Son of God and the Savior of mankind requires extraordinary evidence. And the evidence that Jesus lived, is the son of God and rose from the dead is astonishing, brought down through history by many art forms. But the main source of that proof is the Bible. No other 'sacred writing' has such perfectly accurate predictions of the future and incredible eyewitness accounts. The truth always holds up under scrutiny, and the Bible is the most scrutinized, analyzed, closely examined written work ever created.

Between 1450 BC and 430 BC (when the Old Testament was written) many predictions of the future were recorded by God's prophets. Of the events that were predicted to occur by now, every one has come true exactly the way the prophets foretold they would. The Bible's prophecies (written down many years before they were fulfilled) came true in such a magnificently detailed way that they could not have been predicted by chance.

The quantity of New Testament material is overwhelming compared with other works of antiquity. The average ancient secular work survives on only a handful of manuscripts. Over 20,000 known manuscripts document the writings in the New Testament *alone*. No other work in all of the world's ancient literature enjoys such a wealth of good textual attestation as the New Testament.

These manuscripts were written in *different languages* by people of *different backgrounds, cultures* and *nationalities*. In spite of all these variables, the New Testament texts *all agree*. All the authors spoke without contradiction about one unfolding story—God's redemption of mankind.

The Bible was written by over 40 authors living on three separate continents over a span of 1500 years, and covers hundreds of contentious subjects. Most of these were eyewitness accounts of one profound event. The Bible uses the unity of sixty-six books, all written in different literary styles, but all with one central theme—that of Jesus Christ, Son of God and Savior of mankind.

The Bible is the most relevant, practical and sufficient book for every generation that has ever been written. It is the best selling book of all time. The greatest literary work ever compiled has a solution to every one of our problems. The knowledge of Scripture empowers me, and the beautiful poetry of this miraculous masterpiece comforts me.

All evidence points to the Gospels as trustworthy documents. The gospels were recorded long before legend could corrupt their validity. Documents describe in detail the Divine claims made by Jesus, and substantiate these claims so graphically as to completely overturn the theology of His Jewish audience. He demonstrated that He was the Lord, the Messiah and the Savior of the world, which was not an easy thing to do. He did this by performing miracles which no ordinary man could perform.

The disciples were in a unique position to know whether the Resurrection happened or not, and they went to their deaths proclaiming it to be true. They had absolutely no motive to lie about Jesus and his revelations. They had everything to lose and nothing to gain by following Him, and yet they committed themselves to Him anyway. Nobody willingly dies for a lie. Nobody, *including Christ's enemies,* disclaimed what what written about him.

Albert Einstein, one of the greatest scientists of all time, when asked if he accepted the historical existence of Jesus, replied, "Unquestionably! No one can read the Gospels without feeling the actual presence of Jesus. His personality pulsates in every word. No myth is filled with such life." (*Einstein,* by Walter Isaacson, 2007)

Christianity is the only religion with an overwhelming amount of historical evidence. Objective *facts* from both archaeology and non-Christian writers confirm that the Bible (both the Old and New Testaments) is an authentic historical document. There is an integrity and consistency throughout the Bible that defies natural explanations.

Secular history supports the Bible and provides overwhelming evidence substantiating the fact that the Gospels' stories about Jesus Christ are true. His name is the demarcation line for all record keeping. We honor His birth, death, and resurrection as holidays.

Numerous non-Christian scholars have picked apart the earliest evidence of Jesus, and through their studies and research they have reached the same conclusions—that it's true, and many came to believe in Him. Christian apologist (defender of Biblical truths) and author of 77 books, Josh McDowell, tells us that, "After personally trying to shatter the historicity and validity of the Scriptures, I have come to the conclusion that they are historically trustworthy."

In *Letters From a Skeptic*, Dr. Gregory A. Boyd uses the example of someone in your house yelling, "Fire, fire!" You can either choose to believe him and escape, or you can choose to not believe, and take the chances of being burned alive. Using a different metaphor, we can say that we are all on a train heading with ever-increasing speed toward a cliff. We're not sure when we will come to the edge, but we are certain that we will. Then, at some point along the way, someone intervenes, reporting that what we believe will affect whether we survive the derailment. The most reasonable thing to do is to believe, *especially if the evidence is strong*. The risk of not believing is far greater than the risk of believing. If the information is false, we've lost nothing but our pride. In believing, there is no loss, but we have everything to gain.

Contempt Prior to Investigation

Some people hate Christianity. These people usually know very little about it, and many haven't even given it a good hard look. I ask these people to just check it out before turning away. Christianity offers too much not to consider believing.

There are many ways to seek Him out. Recommended ways to begin our journey are: to go to another Christian; read the Bible or preferably go to a Bible study; find a good church; and finally, add prayer as daily habit. There is a common prayer that anyone can say if they want to develop a personal relationship with Him. It goes like this:

Dear Lord Jesus, I know that I am a sinner and need Your forgiveness. I believe that You died for my sins. I want to turn from my sins. I now invite You to come into my heart and life. I want to trust and follow You as Lord and Savior. In Jesus' name. Amen.

With Jesus Christ in my heart, I have 'a peace that passes all understanding.' I have insight, power and a kind of joy that few religions can duplicate. When I say I'm a Christian, I'm not bragging about my clean living. Being a Christian doesn't mean I'm exempt from wrongdoing. I can only say that I was lost, but now I'm found and forgiven. I've never regretted my decision to follow Him, and I know of no one else who has either. God is able to help me in direct proportion to the degree that I come to Him. The closer I am to Him, the more happiness I have in my life.

Act as If

If you've decided that you want to believe, but you don't know how, one way to encourage faith is to seek Him out. And one way to seek Him is to 'act as if.' Pray about it, go to church, open the Bible...but not just once. Keep praying. And if you don't like the first church, keep trying different ones until you find the one that works for you.

For me, my clarity of thought is in direct proportion to my connection with God. The better my relationship with Him, the better my life seems to be. It stands to reason that if I want to improve my relationship with Him and satisfy my longing for Him, I need to seek Him out in places where I know I'll find Him. Therefore, the best ways to renew our connection with Him are through prayer, fellowship and studying His Word.

Many years ago, Dr. James T. Fisher, one of the country's foremost psychiatrists at the time, wrote *A Few Buttons Missing: The Case Book of a Psychiatrist*. In it, he says: "If you were to take the sum total of all the authoritative articles on the subject of mental hygiene, if you were to combine them and refine them and cleave out the excess verbiage, if you were to take the whole of the meat and none of the parsley, and if you were to have these unadulterated bits of pure scientific knowledge concisely expressed by the most capable of living poets, you would have an awkward and incomplete summation of the Sermon on the mount."

For a person blessed with an exuberant EGO (**E**asing **G**od **O**ut), regular doses of God's Word helps me to remember to follow in His path, not mine. I often need to be reminded that I don't run the show. For that reason, my mind needs to be saturated with His Word as often as possible.

Even though the Christian Church is at the center of human history, it is still misunderstood by many. The Church is the community founded by Christ for the purpose of disseminating His message and bringing people to Him. It is not the best people in the neighborhood gathered together to pat each other on the back, but people who recognize that one of their great needs is forgiveness, and so gather together to find answers by worship of God and fellowship with one another.

Of all the reasons for not going to church, the most common one that is given is, "People who go to church are just a bunch of hypocrites." When people add this to their excuse train, I tell them that I am far from perfect, and I know it. I don't go because I'm perfect, I go because I'm imperfect. I just want to be a better person. It has nothing to do with hypocrisy. It's taken Bill and me a lot of years to realize the importance of growing spiritually, but today we know that we *need* church if we are to grow closer to Him.

I've got a Good Memory—It's Just Short

Church is a rich resource in my effort to live a decent life. Church reminds me and encourages me to witness, so that others may be transformed. Unless I am reminded on a regular basis, I forget that God is available to help me with my life journey. Just like I go to the gym to stay in shape physically, I go to church to stay in shape spiritually. It is not an exhibition, but a foundation; a hospital for our soul, not an arena for entertainment.

Church teaches us to separate ourselves on a regular basis from things that contaminate our relationship with Him. It increases our commitment to virtuous behavior—kindness, generosity, unselfishness and love. Attending church is an easy way for us to show our gratitude to God through worship and prayer.

Let God be thanked there is on Earth an institution that... transcends race, nation and class; an institution which is loyally undertaking to embody the spirit of Christ, and in His name to relieve human suffering, promote human welfare and carry on a ministry of reconciliation among men.

— Dr. Ernest Fremont Tittle
(*Keys to Happiness*, The Reader's Digest Association)

I like to Place Myself in Situations that will Bring Out the Best in Me

I used to think that church was for old people, who only attended because they had nothing else to do, but that's not it at all. They attend because they've lived long enough to know what helps, what works, and what's good. Besides that, I need to be with other believers in order to focus correctly and keep a proper perspective. In the weekly message, my pastor explains profound truths and difficult-to-understand ideas so that I can better appreciate God.

Early in my marriage, my husband and I got away from going to church because we were 'too busy.' Too hip, slick and cool for Sunday School. The choice to attend was finally ours, and we declined, finding better things to do—or so we thought. After the kids were born, I started back *for the kids*. It was good for *them*. Today, I go to church for *me*. It helps me continue to learn. It's a place I can dump my worries and unnecessary burdens I've picked up all week.

Church provides threads of continuity when it seems like the world is falling apart. It's a weekly reminder to continually adjust my journey to harmonize with God's plan. Hope is an important aspect of our being which life tends to eat away unless it is replenished. One way of replenishing hope is by being in the company of hopeful people.

There's nowhere on Earth to find more hopeful people than in a church congregation. Another way to encourage hope is to find someone who needs something. When I get into action, I find my own personal hope is on the road to recovery again. There are always people at church with prayer requests, so you have at your fingertips a list of people who could use your help. I also go to church because I love to hear the stories of faith. Hearing these encourages me to strengthen mine.

Church helps me tether my self-will, because I know that rebellion against God always brings negative things into my life. Church is a source of encouragement in a world where the majority of people are nonbelievers, or weak believers. Church provides an avenue for my journey out of me and into the community of man. It guides me in my decision-making. It helps my judgment. Church offers every aid to help me live well, and cultivates my understanding of God. It allows me to stop and ask myself, "How am I doing as a human being?"

Going to church reminds me in a strange way of when I used to walk into my son's room in the dark. Everything looked all right with the lights off, but then I tweaked the dimmer on the wall up a notch. Things came into focus that I couldn't see before. Touching the dimmer again, I realized that there was more to be discovered, and much more work to be done.

The same thing can be said about church attendance. Without church, I think I'm doing okay, but I'm really just guessing about so many things. Going to church illuminates the way for me. Church 'turns on a light' that enables me to see what needs to be cleaned out in my life. It coaxes me to confront matters which, in the humdrum of daily life, I tend to ignore.

Let's look at those four components of our life again. There is the physical part, which we nourish everyday by getting the proper amount of sleep and good nutrition, exercising and keeping our bodies clean. Our emotional needs are met with hugs, kisses, outward signs of affection and giving and receiving love, and socially, our needs are met by getting involved with other people via organizations, clubs, or just chatting with our neighbors every now and then. We exercise our mental capacities by reading, writing and solving our daily problems. That leaves the spiritual part of our lives. Spiritual growth requires nourishment. I pray, surround myself with other Christians and study His word, because I want to keep the spiritual dimension of 'me' healthy.

Everyone has a spiritual dimension, but because there is a tendency to believe that it can be set aside without immediate, blatant repercussions, we tend to ignore it. Left unnurtured, it shrivels up and rots, just like a pumpkin left on the porch too long.

As a teacher is no better than the effort she puts into teaching, or a skater into skating, so am I no better at being with God than the effort I put into actively seeking Him.

The vast architectures of all the great churches of the world link me to the generations who have come before me. Great hymns remind me of the millions of people who have repeated the same words. When I sing and pray with others, losing myself in the beautiful words, I find that I am caught up in something profoundly significant. Together, my congregation utilizes our strengths, and compensates for any of our deficiencies.

When I pray, I plug into an infinite energy source for peace, harmony and freedom. When praying, I can pitifully whine, or be my most pathetic. Prayer also creates a catharsis, and gives me relief.

The fact that God chose to reveal Himself in Jesus Christ is the uniqueness of Christianity, and the reason Jesus is the preeminent person in history and the cornerstone of my life. My salvation depends on my acceptance of Jesus Christ as my savior. That's it. It's that simple. My eternal life is at stake here.

There is no comfort greater than the comfort I feel knowing that there is something beautiful at the end of the long highway of life, and not just nothingness.

There is no greater hope than the hope that a better day is coming, and believing in Christ as my savior gives me hope that will keep me going, even when there is no other hope.

I thank God every day for providing this space in my book to testify that I love the Lord with all my heart. If you have found yourself in a bad spot, don't break your mind trying to understand it. Just talk to a Christian, and ask how you can get involved.

Try this for a month. Spend time going out and helping people with projects like 'Habitat for Humanity' and local thrift stores and social programs. I don't promise all the answers will come to you, because all of them never will, but I do promise that you will find you can sleep a little better, that a weekend will become more than just time off, and that you just might find that you have a friend in Jesus.

Living in the Sweet Spot

A sweet spot is a place where a combination of factors comes together to create a particularly desirable situation. For example, when used in sports, it means the best place on the bat for optimal impact. For me, the sweet spot of life is where I am most effective in all my relationships. These include my interpersonal relationships, my inner harmony (between my heart, mind and soul), my balance between work and play, and my personal relationship with God.

In my life, I've gone from a very bad spot, where death was a real possibility, to a very sweet spot, where I'm living one of the best lives imaginable and helping others to do the same. I have a better understanding of what's important, and a keener sense of people's pain.

I've gone from terrible heartache to untamable joy, and what I've learned is that life's battles can spur awesome growth. I can take what weather lies ahead, and embrace the challenges it presents me. I can bow to the breezes of life without breaking. I am no longer being battered from one shore to the next, powerless as to my destination.

There was a time when I worried about what clubs I belonged to, what awards hung on my wall, and I wanted to write books to feel important. All these things are laughable now.

The bottom line is, it's our choice how well we will live. The decision to grow is up to us. Only we can decide whether our journey will be enjoyable, whether we'll be a victim or a victor. Having said that, here are my six suggestions for living happy, joyful and free on a regular basis:

Open your Heart to God and Glorify Him in All You Do

When we do this, the rest of my suggestions flow naturally, and are infinitely easier to follow. With a close connection with God, we reap the benefit of His daily comfort and wise counsel. No matter how rough the road becomes, or even if we lose our way, He will carry us safely home.

With God at the helm, it is difficult for other people, places or things to grab hold of us or steer us off course. By having His well-defined sense of direction, discipline and commitment, we are infinitely fortified to craft our lives and our souls into something worthwhile. Following His way affords us the ability to float freely through a God-guided life. My will, rightly directed, provides me with infinite Divine possibilities, and I am truly exhilarated by my ever-changing, constantly unfolding existence.

I've been rich, and I've been poor. I've been up, and I've been *way* down. I've been sick, and I've been well. I've been young, and now I'm not so young. But I have found that God is the solution, regardless of my circumstances. He has become to me so real, present and undeniable, that to do anything less than follow Him would be impossible.

And so I urge you to have the best possible life you can by being a believer, an all the way believer in God, in life and in yourself. My prayer is that God will water the seeds of faith I've planted for you, and that the glory and honor will be His. And by so doing, you will go beyond the mediocre, surpass the average and meet your full potential.

Be Grateful Every Moment, Hour and Day of Your Life

When our vision becomes clouded with discouragement, gratitude buys us a new pair of glasses. Gratitude lets us see the good things in our lives we couldn't see before, or forgot were even there. But it's not about forcing this feeling. It's about paying attention to our life in a different way. It's about mining the pleasures and satisfactions in each day. At times, this may be difficult, but the rewards outweigh the effort. God has given us everything we need to reach our full potential. If we can't find anything to be grateful for, we can be grateful for that.

It is important to make a point of being thankful when good things happen to us, for there is no downside to gratitude. I find gratitude epiphanies in every average, ho-hum day. I go through each day silently praising the Lord when even the tiniest of blessings occurs.

Every day I have tremendous gratitude that God has lifted me from the 'guttermost' to the uttermost, from a life filled with incomprehensible demoralization to a life filled with extraordinary rewards. I am grateful on a daily basis that I have accepted God into my life when I may not have, had things been different. Today, my greatest weaknesses and liabilities have become my greatest assets, and I am thankful that I am a much better person than I could have been.

Find Your Passion and Make a Plan

It's our spiritual, ethical and moral obligation to make full use of the talents and skills we've been blessed with so that we can position ourselves to share our wealth with the world. Therefore, be a good steward of your time, talent and treasure. Take care of yourself, use your time wisely, and cultivate your passion.

Many people spend more time planning a vacation than they do planning their lives. When we ignore our passion, we become like hamsters on treadmills, mindlessly doing the same thing day in, day out, not caring what direction we're headed. Without a plan, we're a victim of our circumstances, and we miss all the immediate benefits (i.e., enthusiasm and motivation) from doing what we love. In short, if we don't prepare for our future, someone or something else will.

We are put here to not only survive life's trials, but through them, to find our deeper purpose. With a profound purpose, we have vitality, and we are vibrantly alive. After a painful event, many overcome their suffering by responding to a greater calling or stronger purpose. A personal mission statement can keep us focused. It can help us add or subtract what is important and what is not from our daily activities.

By centering our lives on correct principles and creating a balanced focus between doing and increasing our ability to do, we become empowered in the task of creating effective, useful, and peaceful lives...for ourselves and our posterity.

— Steven Covey
(The Seven Habits of Highly Effective People)

With only an ill-defined plan or unrealistic goals to guide us, many of us will succumb to frustration, exhaustion, or even self-destruction. Deficiency of foresight and determination will lead us to live myopically, oppressed by today's problems. But once we've found our passion and made a plan, we won't waste our time pursuing meaningless activities that don't enhance our sense of purpose. We'll view each day with wide open eyes filled with expectation, wonder, and joy.

By focusing on the greater purpose for our life, we can really appreciate all the richness this world has to offer, and are less apt to be overwhelmed by minutiae. By keeping an eye on our life as a whole, we can see when things get out of whack. We can correct our course as need be in order to maintain balance and harmony.

Be Determined to get Positive Results Out of Even the Most Negative Experiences

Nothing bad ever happens without equal or greater benefit in return.

— Napoleon Hill

We cannot experience life without loss, but we can control our translation of the event and how we deal with it. Tragedy will leave us either diminished or enhanced. By finding the blessing, we can use our recoveries for our advantage.

Problems challenge us to reach a little higher and dig a little deeper. Painful events enhance our ability to share other people's troubles, and to gain empathy, and patience. By looking for the potential in every setback, each experience will serve as an enhancement in our lives. When we realize that we are going through something terrible for a reason, we have hope. With the belief that in every trial there is a seed of greater benefit, I cannot help but learn from the experience and have hope for the future. Hope automatically reduces our suffering, and is a loyal friend of joy.

By looking for the hidden gift, we take the power out of trouble, and build ourselves up at the same time. When this gift is obscured, sometimes a sense of humor can change our perspective. Laughing at ourselves is a mature coping mechanism and a great stress buster. It bridges the gap between our goal of perfection and the reality of imperfection.

We alone decide whether our life is a comedy or a drama. A good giggle can be a lifesaver. It enhances life, and promotes an atmosphere for learning. Humor has the power to turn a negative situation into a powerful situation. By poking fun at common dilemmas, we build confidence. It brings us closer to others, and a sense of humor even has the power to somehow open doors for us. Even in the worst of times, we can find humor somewhere on a day-to-day basis. Remember, there are no bad days—only good days and growth days.

We all have a certain amount of struggling to do. Even though we cannot always control what happens to us, we *can* still control our responses. This means that our own decisions and behavior help determine whether the day's activities will be a barely remembered fragment of time, an occasion for lingering pain, or an opportunity for growth.

We grow by choosing to grow. We grow by confronting, resisting and reaching, rather than waiting and reacting. We are growing when we are increasingly capable of accepting ourselves for who we are, and taking responsibility for our actions.

We are growing when we increasingly realize our potential, and increasingly enjoy self-fulfillment.

Tragedy hammers home some truths. We can listen to others about tragedy's profound truths, but it's hard to internalize them until they've happened to us. For that reason, not all of us will regain happiness, and not all of us will get better. The challenge is to move from knowledge of the principles of recovery to actual implementation. At first, we need to constantly remind ourselves, until these ideas turn to habits. By reinforcing this practice of expecting positive outcomes on a regular basis, we train our physical, mental, emotional and spiritual muscles for the unavoidable category 5 hurricanes of life.

Offer More Kindness than Necessary to Everybody Around You

People will forget what you said, people will forget what you did, but people will never forget how you made them feel.

— Maya Angelou

There is no better living than when we use our gifts to bless the lives of others. One of the greatest blessings I have in my life today is being in a position to lighten the load for someone else. It is so easy to leave an indelible mark of kindness that it would be ridiculous not to. Get out of yourself, help others and practice large-heartedness.

One of the greatest gifts a person can possess is to be able to reach past the shortcomings of another and find goodness within them. Be kind to unkind people…they probably need it the most, for many of us are fighting a very hard battle indeed. Extend yourself to the last, the lost and the least, for we cannot light another's path without brightening our own. Remember, one surefire way to find joy is to bring joy to others.

If we are kind, nourishing, and loving inside, we'll attract others who mirror that kindness, nourishment and love. Kindness is contagious. When we are kind, we teach others to act the same. We collect people with the same values, further enhancing our life. People want to be around us. They want to be like us. This makes it easy to balance self-concern with other concern. So, live so that those around you flourish, and keep expanding your reach in greater circles of influence.

Leave an Enduring Legacy of Good

Today, I'm positioned to give the gift of wisdom gleaned from years of daily recoveries. I have been over a good portion of the road that all of us travel. I know where it is rough and difficult, and where it is level and easy, and I can now possibly ease the way for someone else.

An old man going down a lone highway
Came in the evening cold and gray
To a chasm vast and deep and wide
Through which was flowing a sullen tide.

171

The old man crossed in the twilight dim;
That swollen stream held no fears for him;
But he turned when safe on the other side
And built a bridge to span the tide.

'Old man,' said a fellow pilgrim near,
'You are wasting your strength with building here;
Your journey will end with the ending day;
You never again must pass this way;
You have crossed the chasm deep and wide—
Why build you this bridge at the eventide?'

The builder lifted his old gray head
'Good friend, in the path I have come,' he said,
'There followeth after me today
A youth whose feet must pass this way,
This swollen stream which was naught to me
To that fair-haired youth may a pitfall be;
He, too, must cross in the twilight dim
Good friend, I am building the bridge for him.'

— Will Allen Dromgoole, *The Bridge Builder*

As it is so beautifully condensed in the Twelve-step program of Alcoholics Anonymous, 'Carry the message, not the mess.' Our lives will serve as an example of victimized lethargy, lack of direction, and continued setbacks, or as an example of a disciplined, God-centered and purpose-driven life.

By reaching out to make a difference in the lives of your family, friends, and community, setting an example for them to do the same, you can leave a lasting legacy and heritage of great value. Your helping or guiding someone else in essence touches many more, since those who you touch will want to do the same. So, be a courageous, competent and contagious encouragement to everybody you encounter.

It has been difficult for me to come forward with my profound inner struggles, but I knew from experience that there must be others with the same challenges. I couldn't be the only person on Earth who suffered the way I did, and I needed to show how recovery was not only possible, but also quite rewarding. Sharing my story is one of the positives I've gleaned from my troubles. I figured that if I could find joy, anybody could, and I could quite possibly teach them how. *Recovering Me, Discovering Joy* is the platform from which, every day, I take off and soar. May you do the same, and may God bless you and yours.

Appendix

Symptoms of Depression*

One of the most recognized symptoms of depression is a profound feeling of sadness, hopelessness, or emptiness. In general, if you've been experiencing some combination of the following emotional or physical symptoms for more than two weeks, and it clearly interferes with your life, discuss your concerns with your doctor:

Emotional

- Sadness throughout the day, nearly every day
- Loss of interest in or enjoyment of your favorite activities
- Feelings of emptiness or hopelessness
- Feeling stressed, nervous, or overwhelmed
- Trouble concentrating or making decisions
- Feelings of worthlessness
- Excessive or inappropriate feelings of guilt
- Irritability or restlessness
- Thoughts of death or suicide

Physical

- Fatigue or lack of energy
- Sleeping too much or too little
- Change in appetite or weight
- Aches and pains
- Headache
- Back pain
- Digestive problems
- Dizziness

Don't let this list of symptoms scare you. Treatments and therapies are available that can help ease and even eliminate the emotional and physical symptoms of depression.

*Courtesy of: http://www.cymbalta.com

Symptoms of Social Phobia

(Social Anxiety Disorder)*

According to the DSM (The Diagnostic and Statistical Manual of Mental Disorders), "The essential feature of Social Phobia is a marked and persistent fear of social or performance situations in which embarrassment may occur." (p. 450) The following specific diagnostic criteria are reproduced verbatim (except for codings and page references) from the DSM-IV TR (where 'IV TR' indicates fourth edition, text revision), page 456.

Social phobia is an intense fear of becoming humiliated in social situations, specifically of embarrassing yourself in front of other people. It often runs in families and may be accompanied by depression or alcoholism. Social phobia often begins around early adolescence or even younger.

If you suffer from social phobia, you tend to think that other people are very competent in public and that you are not. Small mistakes you make may seem to you much more exaggerated than they really are. Blushing itself may seem painfully embarrassing, and you feel as though all eyes are focused on you. You may be afraid of being with people other than those closest to you. Or your fear may be more specific, such as feeling anxious about giving a speech, talking to a boss or other authority figure, or dating. The most common social phobia is a fear of public speaking. Sometimes social phobia involves a general fear of social situations such as parties. More rarely it may involve a fear of using a public restroom, eating out, talking on the phone, or writing in the presence of other people, such as when signing a check.

Although this disorder is often thought of as shyness, the two are not the same. Shy people can be very uneasy around others, but they don't experience the extreme anxiety in anticipating a social situation, and they don't necessarily avoid circumstances that make them feel self-conscious. In contrast, people with social phobia aren't necessarily shy at all. They can be completely at ease with people most of the time, but particular situations, such as walking down an aisle in public or making a speech, can give them intense anxiety. Social phobia disrupts normal life, interfering with career or social relationships. For example, a worker can turn down a job promotion because he can't give public presentations. The dread of a social event can begin weeks in advance, and symptoms can be quite debilitating.

People with social phobia are aware that their feelings are irrational. Still, they experience a great deal of dread before facing the feared situation, and they may go out of their way to avoid it. Even if they manage to confront what they fear, they usually feel very anxious beforehand and are intensely uncomfortable throughout. Afterwards, the unpleasant feelings may linger, as they worry about how they may have been judged or what others may have thought or observed about them.

Specific Symptoms of this Disorder:

A marked and persistent fear of one or more social or performance situations in which the person is exposed to unfamiliar people or to possible scrutiny by others. The individual fears that he or she will act in a way (or show anxiety symptoms) that will be humiliating or embarrassing.

Note: In children, there must be evidence of the capacity for age-appropriate social relationships with familiar people and the anxiety must occur in peer settings, not just in interactions with adults.

Exposure to the feared social situation almost invariably provokes anxiety, which may take the form of a situationally bound or situationally predisposed Panic Attack.

Note: In children, the anxiety may be expressed by crying, tantrums, freezing, or shrinking from social situations with unfamiliar people.

The person recognizes that the fear is excessive or unreasonable.

Note: In children, this feature may be absent.

The feared social or performance situations are avoided or else are endured with intense anxiety or distress.

The avoidance, anxious anticipation, or distress in the feared social or performance situation(s) interferes significantly with the person's normal routine, occupational (academic) functioning, or social activities or relationships, or there is marked distress about having the phobia.

*Courtesy of psychcentral.com

Are You An Alcoholic?

Ask yourself the following questions and answer them as honestly as you can.

	YES	NO
1. Do you lose time from work due to drinking?	O	O
2. Is drinking making your home life unhappy?	O	O
3. Do you drink because you are shy with other people?	O	O
4. Is drinking affecting your reputation?	O	O
5. Have you ever felt remorse after drinking?	O	O
6. Have you gotten into financial difficulties as a result of drinking?	O	O
7. Do you turn to lower companions and an inferior environment when drinking?	O	O
8. Does your drinking make you careless of your family's welfare?	O	O
9. Has your ambition decreased since drinking?	O	O
10. Do you crave a drink at a definite time of day?	O	O
11. Do you want a drink the next morning?	O	O
12. Does drinking cause you to have difficulty in sleeping?	O	O
13. Has your efficiency decreased since drinking?	O	O
14. Is drinking jeopardizing your job or business?	O	O
15. Do you drink to escape from worries or trouble?	O	O
16. Do you drink alone?	O	O
17. Have you ever had a complete loss of memory as a result of drinking?	O	O
18. Has your physician ever treated you for drinking?	O	O
19. Do you drink to build up your self-confidence?	O	O
20. Have you ever been to a hospital or institution on account of drinking?	O	O

If you have answered YES to any one of the questions, there is a definite warning that you may be an alcoholic.

If you have answered YES to any two, the chances are that you are an alcoholic.

If you have answered YES to three or more, you are definitely an alcoholic.

(These questions were made up by Dr. Robert V. Seliger for use at John Hopkins University Hospital, Baltimore, MD, in deciding whether a patient is alcoholic.) Copyright © Recovered Alcoholic Clergy Association, 2000

The 12 Suggested Steps of Alcoholics Anonymous

1. We admitted we were powerless over alcohol—that our lives had become unmanageable.

2. Came to believe that a Power greater than ourselves could restore us to sanity.

3. Made a decision to turn our will and our lives over to the care of God as we understood Him.

4. Made a searching and fearless moral inventory of ourselves.

5. Admitted to God, to ourselves and to another human being the exact nature of our wrongs.

6. Were entirely ready to have God remove all these defects of character.

7. Humbly asked Him to remove our shortcomings.

8. Made a list of all persons we had harmed, and became willing to make amends to them all.

9. Made direct amends to such people wherever possible, except when to do so would injure them or others.

10. Continued to take personal inventory and when we were wrong promptly admitted it.

11. Sought through prayer and meditation to improve our conscious contact with God, as we understood Him, praying only for knowledge of His will for us and the power to carry that out.

12. Having had a spiritual awakening as the result of these steps, we tried to carry this message to alcoholics, and to practice these principles in all our affairs.

From:

ALCOHOLICS ANONYMOUS
The Story of How many Thousands of Men and Women Have Recovered from Alcoholism, NEW AND REVISED EDITION (Second Edition)
ALCOHOLICS ANONYMOUS PUBLISHING, INC.
NEW YORK CITY, 1955, pp. 59–60

The Promises Of Alcoholics Anonymous

"If we are painstaking about this phase of our development, we will be amazed before we are half way through. We are going to know a new freedom and a new happiness. We will not regret the past nor wish to shut the door on it. We will comprehend the word serenity and we will know peace. No matter how far down the scale we have gone, we will see how our experience can benefit others. That feeling of uselessness and self-pity will disappear. We will lose interest in selfish things and gain interest in our fellows. Self-seeking will slip away. Our whole attitude and outlook upon life will change. Fear of people and of economic insecurity will leave us. We will intuitively know how to handle situations which used to baffle us. We will suddenly realize that God is doing for us what we could not do for ourselves.

Are these extravagant promises? We think not. They are being fulfilled among us–sometimes quickly, sometimes slowly. They will always materialize if we work for them."

Selected Bibliography

Alcoholics Anonymous. Alcoholics Anonymous Publishing, Inc. New York City, 1955.

Breathnach, Sarah Ban. *Simple Abundance.* New York: Warner Books, 1998.

C., Chuck. *A New Pair of Glasses.* Irvine, CA: New-Look Publishing Company, 1984.

Carey, Dave. *The Ways We Choose.* Wilsonville, Oregon: Book Partners, 2000.

Covey, Steven R. *The Seven Habits of Highly Effective People.* New York: Simon & Schuster, 1989.

De Becker, Gavin. *The Gift of Fear.* Little, Brown & Co. 1997.

Drummond, Edward H., M.D. *Overcoming Anxiety without Tranquilizers.* Dutton: 1997.

Erikson, E. H. *Young Man Luther: A Study in Psychoanalysis and History.* New York: W. W. Norton & Co., 1958.

Fletcher, William M. *The Triumph of Surrender.* Colorado Springs, Co: Nav Press, 1987.

Harrell, Keith. *Attitude is Everything – 10 Life-changing steps to turning attitude into action.* HarperCollins Publishers, Inc., N.Y., N.Y. 2000.

Jordan, William George. *The Majesty of Calmness.* New York: Pyramid Publications, Inc., 1966.

Kersey, Cynthia. *Unstoppable.* Naperville, IL: Sourcebooks, Inc., 1998.

Keys to Happiness. Pleasantville, N.Y: The Reader's Digest Association, 1955.

Lauer, Robert & Jeanette, Ph.D. *Watersheds Mastering Life's Unpredictable Crises.* Boston: Little, Brown & Co., 1988.

Life Application Bible, New International Version, Wheaton, IL: Tyndale House Publishers, Inc. & Grand Rapids, MI: Zondervan Publishing House, 1991.

Lydon, Susan Gordon. *Take the Long Way Home.* San Francisco: Harper, 1993.

McDowell, Josh. *Evidence that Demands a Verdict.* San Bernardino, CA: Here's Life Publishers, Inc., 1979.

Markway, Barbara G. Ph.D., *Dying of Embarrassment.* Oakland, CA: New Harbinger Publications, Inc., 1992.

Marshall, John R., M.D., *Social Phobia.* New York: Basic Books, 1994.

Monroe, Judy. *Phobias.* New Jersey: Enslow Publishers, 1996.

Morin, Richard A. M.D. *Masquerade, Unmasking Dual Diagnosis.* Portland, OR: Arnica Publishing, Inc., 2004.

Morley, Pat. *The Man in the Mirror.* Nashville, TN: Thomas Nelson Publishers, 1992.

Naylor, Thomas H. *The Search for Meaning.* Nashville, TN: Abingdon Press, 1994.

Nightingale, Earl. *The Strangest Secret.* Niles, IL: Nightingale Covent Audiotape, 1957.

Nozick, Robert. *The Examined Life.* NY, NY: Simon & Schuster, 1989.

Peale, Norman Vincent. *Why Some Positive Thinkers Get Positive Results.* NY, NY: Random House.

Peck, M. Scott. *The Road Less Traveled.* New York: Touchstone, 1978.

Schuller, Robert H. *My Journey.* San Francisco: Harper, 2001.

Sheehan, George. *Running Blind.* Clayton, Vic: Warner Books, 1978.

Twelve Steps and Twelve Traditions. New York City: Alcoholics Anonymous World Services, Inc., 1952.

Waitley, Denis. *Seeds of Greatness.* New Jersey: Fleming H. Revell Co., 1983.

Wholey, Dennis. *The Miracle of Change.* New York: Pocket Books, 1997.

Yepsen, Roger B., Jr. *How to Boost Your Brain Power.* Emmaus, PN: Rodale Press, 1987.

Zubko, Andy. *Treasury of Spiritual Wisdom.* San Diego, CA: Blue Dove Press.

www.beliefnet.com

www.clarifyingchristianity.com

www.cymbalta.com

www.gospeloutreach.net

www.psychcentral.com

Index